JUMPING ON THE CALIPHATE CARAVAN

Overview Of The Jihadi Bandwagon Effect Traversing Asia And Africa

By Sandra Warmoth

CENTER FOR SECURITY POLICY PRESS

Jumping on the Caliphate Caravan:
Overview of the Jihadi Bandwagon Effect Traversing Asia and Africa
is published in the United States by the Center for Security Policy Press,
a division of the Center for Security Policy.

March 25, 2015

THE CENTER FOR SECURITY POLICY
1901 Pennsylvania Avenue, Suite 201 Washington, DC 20006
Phone: (202) 835-9077 | Email: info@securefreedom.org
For more information, please see securefreedom.org

Book design by Adam Savit
Cover design by Alex VanNess

TABLE OF CONTENTS

INTRODUCTION

A public outcry over beheadings of American journalists by Muslim terrorists spurred the reluctant United States (U.S.) President, Barak Obama on 10 September 2014 to initiate a four-point plan[1] to "degrade and ultimately destroy" the "not Islamic" Islamic State (IS). Notwithstanding, the group continues territorial conquests, forcible imposition of Islamic Law, annihilation of indigenous non-Muslim communities in Syria and Iraq, and is seeking new alliances and outposts in strategic areas of Africa and Asia. Indeed, during his address on U.S. operations against IS, President Obama noted that the greatest emerging threats emanate from the Middle East and North Africa.

This article focuses on selected emerging threats in Asia and in Africa as they present themselves in accordance with the global Islamic agenda. The research finds that the rise of IS and its claim to a revived caliphate[2] is inspiring Muslims around the world, and is emboldening armed non-state Muslim actors in Asia and Africa, including Al'Qaeda (AQ), and energizing their efforts to form subversive Islamic statal entities within their respective spheres of influence. The resurgence of the global jihad movement in Asia and Africa is driving armed conflict in these already unstable, fragile regions and is threatening a cascade of failing states. Spearheading an ambitious effort to dissolve the Western nation-state system and erase borders imposed upon these restive regions per the European colonial Sykes-Picot Agreement of 1916 by exploiting under-governed areas experiencing gaps in capacity and security, IS, AQ, and other jihadist forces sharing similar objectives, despite differences, are advancing their collective goal to unify Islamic governance under one global caliphate ruled by Islamic Law, i.e. shariah.

This report seeks to shed light on this process; and to raise the level of awareness regarding how the 21st century elevation of the Islamic prophet Muhammad's seventh century dictums and deeds are providing justification and motivation behind jihadi military assaults across multiple fronts, and increasingly threatening both regional and global security. Finally, the author suggests that a holistic strategy replace the piecemeal counter-terrorism approach to address the threat, and accordingly contributes several recommendations.

FOCUS ON ASIA

Al-Qa'eda Central's Counter-Caliphate Response to the IS Caliphate

Al-Qa'eda Central (AQC) chief Ayman al-Zawahiri's belated response[3] to the IS June 2014 declaration of a self-proclaimed caliphate[4] in Syria and Iraq and the rendering that all other jihadist entities are invalidated by its establishment[5] was calculated and graduated: (a) snub the breakaway AQ group; (b) release in July 2014 AQ's inaugural online issue, *Al Nafir* or *Call to Arms*[6], which, echoing the late Usama Bin Laden, trumpets this terrorist network's renewed oath of allegiance to Mullah Mohammed Omar, leader of the Afghan Taliban and Islamic Emirate in Afghanistan[7] and commissions AQ branches everywhere to recovering lost territory for the "coming State of the Caliphate;" (c) the September 2014 roll-out of another AQ branch, Qaedat al-Jihad in the Indian Subcontinent (QJIS)[8], with designs on India, Bangladesh, and Burma; proclaim QJIS' loyalty to Omar and venerate him as "Emir of the Believers" – a coveted designation that lends legitimacy to the authority of a qualified caliph or other such sovereign[9]; and issue an Abdullah Azzam-style call-up[10] for jihad to the ummah[11] to "revive its caliphate," apparently beginning on the Indian subcontinent[12]; (d) by extension, in November 2014 – release, via QJIS, an Abdullah Azzam-style call-up for a *fard ayn* jihad[13], emphasizing that it is a global obligation to wage jihad with one's person against the America-led coalition in Iraq and Syria, thus evoking an Islamic legal ruling per the rules of jihad that makes it a *compulsory personal duty* for every Muslim man, woman, and child worldwide to join in the fighting without asking permission in order to "defend" Islam, establish shariah, and support jihadists fighting in this theater; and an appeal to jihadists therein to unify and close ranks – incontrovertibly under the AQ brand with IS in compliance – in order to eliminate the "American aggression."

The lionization of Omar is a rebuke to the IS self-appointed caliph, Abu Bakr al-Baghdadi[14], referred to as "*khalifah* Ibrahim" and considered "leader [emir] for Muslims everywhere" by a growing list of supporters impressed with his qualifications, particularly because he claims descent from the Quraysh tribe of Islam's prophet, Muhammad: the model jihadist[15]. It is an attempt by al-Zawahiri – perceived by some among the newer generations of jihadists to be starchy and presiding over a waning network – to stimulate steadfastness within AQ's ranks as key affiliates like Al-Qa'eda in the Islamic Maghreb (AQIM) grapple with divided loyalties and resultantly lose seasoned jihadists to IS[16]. Whether al-Zawahiri will have enough sway over his far-flung and diffused post-9-11 network to prevent high-level defections to IS remains to be seen. Barring reconciliation per his prescription, al-Zawahiri is signaling that he does not intend to leave the IS caliphate project to progress along its askew course without a robust response from his network.

Progress Report on IS Caliphate Project and Related Security Concerns

Undeterred, al-Baghdadi's caliphate project is pressing ahead, as is his slick media campaign. Some Iraqi officials claimed U.S.-led airstrikes occurring between 7-8 November 2014 injured or killed al-Baghdadi, but once again they were proven wrong[17], and this time IS used the occasion to not only demonstrate its resolve in the face of the attacks, but to deliver a major announcement while it had the attention of a worldwide audience: IS released five audio messages between 9-10 November featuring pledges of allegiance to al-Baghdadi[18], which were followed by a 17-minute audio message that surfaced on 13 November with a male speaker believed to be al-Baghdadi, who contradicted the Iraqi officials' claims[19]. The man delivering the message referenced events that took place following the November airstrikes, and he defiantly used the occasion to announce the expansion of the IS caliphate project into Saudi Arabia, Yemen, Egypt, Libya, and Algeria. Moreover, he announced the nullification of existing Muslim terrorist groups and organizations within those Arab lands – a harbinger, per the June caliphate declaration, that as IS troops roll in, **"the legality of all emirates, groups, states, and organizations become null[20]."** He also accepted the *bay'a* or oath of allegiance from several jihadist collectives and jihadist groups based within these states, thereby demonstrating that IS has a toehold in these areas; and he appointed *wali* to serve as provincial leaders over *wilayah* or provinces designated for IS's newly proclaimed sphere of activity. There was no mention of expansion into Pakistan, Indonesia, the Philippines, or other places where non-Arab factions made similar pledges to al-Baghdadi. That expansion would come later. In December 2014, U.S. officials stated that although other IS top leaders were killed in the U.S.-led airstrikes, al-Bahgdadi was still alive[21].

Concerns mount as the bulk of al-Baghdadi's caliphate project expands from Syria and Iraq outward to the Persian Gulf countries and North Africa. In the Persian Gulf, **concerns over the IS expansion program** include: (1) vulnerability of Saudi Arabia's energy infrastructure and further agitation among the restive Iranian-backed Shi'a populace in the kingdom's oil-rich Eastern Province[22] – concerns heightened by the 5 January 2015 IS attack on a Saudi northern border patrol[23], the 23 January death of Saudi King Abdullah[24] and a potential succession crisis[25], and the 22 January collapse of Yemen's government[26]; (2) further destabilization of Yemen, positioned on the Strait of Bab al-Mandab along a Red Sea oil shipping route in the backyard of the Gulf States, and grappling with the 22 January 2015 resignation of its president and his cabinet[27] amid an AQ insurgency and an Iranian-backed Shi'a rebellion among powerful Houthi tribes; and elevation of domestic Sunni-Shi'a tensions; and (3) a deepening Sunni-Shi'a cleavage triggering widespread violence throughout the region. In North Africa, concerns over the IS expansion program include: (1) a security environment growing more complex and dangerous as Egyptian forces battling jihadists groups in the Sinai increasingly must contend with an IS presence that is energizing this theater and acting as a magnet for foreign jihadists wanting to participate in a long-awaited epic battle to obliterate Jews and to usher in apocalyptic End Time events per Allah's dictates[28] (2) further destabilization of Libya that could tip this failing state over to terrorist state status as it reels under assaults emanating from well-armed alliances of domestic militias seizing and holding strategic territory, a strong AQ presence, and an influx of foreign jihadi groups setting up outposts – some of these groups seeking to establish ties with IS; (3) heightened vulnerability of Algeria and its energy infrastructure[29] as Algerian forces face renewed lethal attacks [30] from the Algerian-rooted, regionally networked core AQIM, which has been fighting[31] to overthrow this state to make it part of a revived caliphate[32], and whose veteran defectors to IS remain in the country[33]; and (4) added vitality to the Islamic insurgency in this sub-region, which would further destabilize the continent.

As an added concern, IS is currently making inroads into Pakistan and Afghanistan, states where AQ is deeply rooted, thereby inching closer to the Indian subcontinent, where al-Zawahiri is operating. IS is going into Pakistan's key cities and refugee camps, where it is distributing booklets written in the local languages, and it is endeavoring to lure AQ and Taliban leaders over to al-Baghdadi[34]. Also, according to Pakistani and U.S. officials, Pakistan-based ex-Guantanamo detainee Abdul Rahim Muslim Dost[35], who swore allegiance to al-Baghdadi, is actively recruiting for IS in Pakistan and Afghanistan[36]. Afghan officials, meanwhile, including an Afghan general and a provincial governor, confirmed for the first time on 12 January 2015 that a man identified as Mullah Abdul Rauf, an ex-Guantanamo detainee[37], was actively recruiting fighters for IS, flying black flags, and according to some sources, including a tribal leader in the strategic Sangin district in the eastern Helmand province, battling Taliban fighters[38]. Gen. Mahmood Khan, deputy commander of the Afghan National Army 215th Corps, which in October 2014 assumed responsibility of camps Leatherneck and Bastion[39] informed that residents in several districts in the southern Helmand province have said that Rauf's representatives are fanning out across the area to recruit people to IS.

As long as there is AQ and IS rivalry, and these terrorist entities remain robust, they are likely to demonstrate their wherewithal and operational capabilities by competitively and progressively launching innovative, daring, and spectacular attacks targeting common enemies in order to score points in the jihadi world, to win Muslims over to their respective caliphate projects, and to command the international limelight.

AQ-IS Cooperation Evolving in the Midst of Their Rivalry

Despite the deadly rivalry between AQ and IS, particularly in Syria between IS and AQ-affiliate Jabhat al-Nusra, and apparently now in Pakistan via IS attacks on the AQ-linked Taliban, cooperation between the two entities is becoming more evident as the jihadi world struggles with overlapping loyalties to AQ and IS, and calls for them to reconcile and unite against the West amid U.S. airstrikes targeting the IS; the so-called Khorasan group, an AQ affiliate; and inadvertently, at least initially, Jabhat al-Nusra[40].

Cooperation between AQ and IS surfaced in August 2014 on the mountains of east Lebanon along the porous border area between Lebanon and Syria, where Jabhat al-Nusra Front and IS militants are hiding. AQ and IS formed a "tactical battlefield alliance," and along with other Syrian rebel groups, they use the area as staging grounds for attacks against Syrian troops and militias loyal to Syrian President Bashar al-Assad in the Qalamoun region north of Damascus, and for abductions and hostage-taking operations targeting Lebanese soldiers in the northwest border town of Arsal[41]. The two groups in August overran Arsal and engaged the Lebanese army in gun battles, then took hostages from the military and police and later executed four of them[42]. Lebanon's state-run National News Agency reported on 20 January 2015 that three more Lebanese men were abducted by IS, which, in the jihadi cost-benefit calculus, indicates that hostage-taking continues to yield good returns for terrorist groups operating in the area, particularly as their other sources of revenue are under attack, so more of this activity can be expected.

Prompted by the targeted airstrikes against IS in northern Iraq, which bolstered this group's popularity in Yemeni jihadi circles, on 14 August 2014 the Yemen-based Al Qaeda in the Arabian Peninsula (AQAP) released a message of solidarity via Twitter that was circuitously directed at the IS: The message, inter alia, spoke of the duty to support the group's efforts against the U.S. airstrikes, and it provided advice on how to navigate enemy attacks, according to a translation by SITE Intelligence Group[43].

The November 2014 U.S. airstrikes against Jabhat al-Nusra and IS reportedly led to "ceasefires and some cooperation at the local level" between these two groups in the interest of fighting "moderate" rebel groups in Syria[44].

On 21 November 2014, senior AQAP member and cleric, Harith bin Ghazi al-Nadhari, rebuked IS over al-Baghdadi's caliphate declaration and its expansion into Yemen; yet, he still expressed hope that divisions between IS and al-Nusra could be healed in Syria and offered hope of future unity between AQAP and IS if al-Baghdadi withdrew his fatwa claiming Yemen for his caliphate[45].

Al-Nadhari was leveraging the Islamic Salafia doctrine of *al-wala' wa'l-bara'*: love for Allah, Islam's prophets, and Muslims, and enmity and hatred toward non-Muslims and the Islamic perception of falsehood[46]. Although IS and AQ are at odds, in the face of a common enemy, this doctrine enables them to reach across the divide. Popular in the jihadi-sphere, deeply ingrained in the educational curriculum in Saudi Arabia, and widely taught among diaspora Muslims, this doctrine was expounded upon by the aforementioned Islamic strategist Abdullah Azzam, who espoused total separation between Muslims and non-Muslims: no sitting together, no living in the same dwelling, no celebrating non-Muslim holidays, no employing non-Muslims, and no accepting judgment under non-Muslim laws [47]. *Al-wala' wa'l-bara'* helps explain why Western counter-terrorism operations with Muslim and Arab countries are typically unreliable and unfruitful, and it may hold the key to future reconciliation between IS and AQ.

The latest occurrence of cooperation between AQ and IS is apparently emerging from the January 2015 sophisticated[48] jihadist attacks in France. A pre-attack video titled, "Soldier of the Caliphate [49]" released 11 January 2015 referencing the 7-9 January jihadi rampage involving the deadly shooting attack on the Charlie Hebdo magazine in Paris [50]; and the fatal shooting of a policewoman in Montrouge in southern Paris, as well as the deadly hostage-taking situation at the Parisian Hyper Casher kosher supermarket[51], sent red flags alerting authorities of possible coordination between AQ and IS. Amedy Coulibaly, the supermarket gunman, claimed allegiance to IS in the video, yet the video lacked the group's usual markings[52], and it is unclear if he had concrete connections to the group or if he was only ideologically endorsing it[53]. Coulibaly made a similar claim of allegiance to IS to CNN affiliate, BFMTV[54]. In the video, Coulibaly took credit for providing money and logistical help to Cherif and Said Kouachi, the French-Algerian brothers who carried out the magazine attack and who said they were working for AQAP. An arms dealer in Brussels known in the underworld turned himself in to local police and confessed to selling arms, ammunition, and a car to Coulibaly, leading to the discovery by federal police of purchase papers and other evidence in the dealer's apartment they say back the confession; while Belgian press reports allege those arms were used by the Kouachi brothers in the Charlie Hebdo attack, and by Coulibaly in the Hyper Casher attack[55]. The Kouachi brothers' claim to be working for AQAP was at least partially verified by the previously mentioned senior AQAP member, al-Nadhari, who confirmed in an audio recording published online 9 January the group's responsibility for the actions of the Kouachi brothers[56]; and by AQAP commander Nasr Ibn Ali al-Ansi in a video that surfaced on 14 January taking credit for the magazine attack on behalf of his group[57]. U.S. and French intelligence officials at this point in their investigations suspect that the attack was inspired by AQ, but not directed by AQAP[58]. Coulibaly demanded freedom for the Kouachi brothers during the supermarket hostage-taking incident[59], and investigators learned that all three perpetrators, and Coulibaly's common-law wife, Hayat Boumeddiene, were close associates plugged into the same terrorist network[60]. Just before the supermarket attack, Coulibaly's common-law wife slipped out of France, and with outside help made her way to Tel Abyad, Syria, which is IS-controlled territory that is a two-hour drive to the IS stronghold, Raqqa[61]. Also, four men were arrested and face charges in France on suspicion of providing logistical support to Coulibaly[62], potentially broadening the scope of the plot. Meanwhile, an audio recording was reportedly released on 26 January 2015 by IS media, Al-Furqan, believed to be the voice of IS spokesman Abu Mohammed al-Adnani, who praised recent attacks on Western soil, including the attack on the Charlie Hebdo magazine, and called on Muslims in Western countries to target Crusaders, a reference to Christians and the Christian West[63].

As the West continues to prosecute a protracted War on Islamic Terrorism, the undertaking, to some measure, is likely to catalyze AQ and IS cooperation. Although AQ and IS are engaged in a bitter rivalry, terrorist groups have a history of cooperating when they feel threatened by internal, regional, and international political and strategic conditions and events, and by states or superpowers[64]. In a drive for survival, terrorist groups forge alliances and augment their capabilities as they cooperate for mutual benefit, which results in increased killing capacity[65]. An example of cooperation between rival terrorist groups can be seen with AQ, a Sunni group, which learned about suicide bombings from Hizb'allah, a Shi'ite group; and their logistical cooperation came to light during the trial of AQ operatives involved in the east Africa embassy bombings in Kenya and Tanzania in 1998[66], which, combined, killed 234 and wounded more than 4,650[67].

Considering the evolution of cooperation discussed in these cases covering August 2014 to January 2015, taken as a whole, according to open sources, there is apparent cooperation, to varying degrees, and at least at varying lower levels, that is taking place between AQ and IS in the following ways: tactical and ideological, and possibly logistical. While tactical cooperation between lower-level AQ and IS operatives, including their sympathizers, will likely continue to occur sporadically, al-wala' wa'l-bara' will likely continue to deepen the duty-to-support sentiment among low- to mid-level members of these two groups, as well as their followers and supporters, as together they contend with a despised enemy using overwhelming firepower. Overall, this dynamic could form the basis for more cooperation at deeper levels which may be broader in scope, and could even have future implications for reconciliation between AQ and IS at the upper level. Before that could happen, AQ would have to overcome two major obstacles: (1) al-Bagdadi's moves to usurp al-Zawahiri's position as the spearhead of global jihad; and (2) fear that IS, in keeping with its predecessor, AQ in Iraq (AQI), may again tarnish the AQ brand as the ongoing brutal IS campaign continues to target Muslims[68]. AQI was an affiliate of AQC, which renamed itself Islamic State of Iraq (ISI), and in May 2010, al-Baghdadi took over ISI[69]. AQI's own brutal insurgency created revulsion in the Islamic world because Muslims were also victims of the group's guerrilla war against coalition forces and their domestic allies[70]. All told, determining factors for cooperation will include whether both of these powerful rivals could hold their own while facing a sustained campaign of enemy fire and whether their respective cost-benefit analyses determine that they do not need to combine their resources and capability. If they make amends at top level, it could be very dangerous, as the symmetrical alliance would involve two very capable partners: AQ with its far-flung, diffused network and enduring old-school ties, and IS with its deep pockets and mission-driven newer-generation appeal. If they determine that they can soldier on alone in their individual caliphate undertakings, then despite pressure in the jihadi world to reconcile, reconciliation may be shelved, at least for a while, in favor of lethal and spectacular competition.

AQ Boosts Old Ties to South and Central Asia Terror Syndicate; Faces IS AfPak Push

When al-Zawahiri established QJIS in September 2014, he formalized AQ's existing networked relationships with seasoned jihadist groups based in Pakistan, Afghanistan, and India. Former U.S. Secretary of Defense Robert Gates in 2010 described this type of networked arrangement as a syndicate in the region[71].

Like mergers, syndicates enable jihadist groups to pool resources in order to increase their lethality and resilience as they advance a common cause.

Mergers involve high-end terrorist group cooperation as the parties fuse together, which greatly expands their capabilities. Mergers occur when the terrorist groups involved realize the power of working together, and when the parties are under assault or being dismantled and must unify to survive. A larger terrorist group, typically the stronger party, may absorb a smaller terrorist group, typically the weaker party, to enable the latter to survive, while the latter may bring to the table special competencies that could be leveraged by the former's infrastructure. A classic merger took place between Usama bin Laden's AQ and Ayman al-Zawahiri's Egyptian Islamic Jihad (EIJ)[72]. The merger was grounded in a mutually beneficial bond that dated back to the mid-1990s in Afghanistan, and it occurred gradually: first with bin Laden financing al-Zawahiri's nearly decimated and cash-strapped EIJ, and then with EIJ's functional and ideological integration into AQ. The merger became Al-Qaedat al-Jihad. During the process, al-Zawahiri swore allegiance to bin Laden and eventually became his deputy, and their cooperation developed at the strategic, operational, and logistical levels. Al Zawahiri, a strategic thinker, brought to the merger EIJ's sophisticated use of suicide attacks and operational experience, and many Egyptian fighters that built the logistical backbone of the AQ network, which these two leaders jointly created. The AQ-EIJ fusion enabled AQ to make its international debut in 1998 with the simultaneous attacks on the U.S. embassies in Nairobi and in Dar es Salaam, which expanded AQ's reach and elevated its profile. Al-Zawahiri, moreover, played a key role in planning the 9-11 attacks. In the post 9-11 environment, he and bin Laden served as the driving force behind the ideology and motivation for global jihad.

Essentially, Black's Law Dictionary[73] describes syndicates as involving associations of individuals formed to conduct and carry out some particular transaction in which the members are mutually interested. By extension, terrorist syndicates may involve associations of terrorist groups and mergers, mobile and stationary resource networks, and criminal, criminalizing, and compromised stakeholders that come together to conduct and carry out mutually beneficial transactions in order to better enable participants to advance non-conflicting objectives across a broad platform. Consequently, terrorist syndicate participants, to varying degrees, have the ability to tap into and leverage their pooled capabilities, competencies and knowledge resources, and financial and intelligence assets. The terrorist syndicate may form associations with other terrorist syndicates, and criminal syndicates, and plug into existing local, regional, and transnational pipelines in order to open up new opportunities, extend reach, and further enhance performance, agility, and resilience.

Formalizing existing networked relationships in Pakistan, Afghanistan, and India in the framework of a terrorist syndicate whose participants – such as Omar's Afghan Taliban – are seasoned jihadist entities is likely to strengthen the foundation of al-Zawahiri's caliphate project going forward.

Another key participant in the terrorist syndicate in this region is the long-established Haqqani insurgent group and resource network (HN), which operates in the AfPak theatre and is the actual, but underreported, "fountainhead" of global jihad[74]. Robust generational ties exist between AQC and the HN, with the latter also committed to the establishment of a caliphate. Incubator for AQ and provider of battlefront access, the HN is adept at enabling call-ups and jihads, as demonstrated during the Afghan war against the former Soviet Union in the 1980s, and during the post-9-11 Afghan war against the NATO-led multinational forces. The HN uses mountainous geography and the shelter of Pakistan's close border to maintain a rear supply base, serving as a logistical facilitator for AQ to launch attacks beneficial to advancing common objectives. An inclusive and pragmatic strategic approach enables the HN to link diverse groups, including state and non-state actors, and its deftness brings fractious and rival terrorist groups into tactical alliances. Such local partnering furthers AQ's aims of bringing many terrorist groups into its fold to advance global jihad. Given is military prowess, the HN is a force multiplier for AQ, strengthening the latter's campaigns and helping fill its ranks with operatives, while the HN uses these fighters for local battles to expand its clout with key actors like the Pakistan's Directorate for Inter-Services Intelligence (ISI).

Longstanding ties also exist between AQC and franchise Tehreek-e-Taliban Pakistan (TTP) aka the Pakistani Taliban, an insurgent umbrella group in the terrorist syndicate. However, these ties are currently being put to the test: The

TTP's fruitless peace talks with the Pakistan government in early 2014 created a rift that caused TTP commanders to bolt, and the TTP to split into three core factions that reiterated allegiance to Omar[75]. By mid 2014, loyalties appeared to be cracking as some media took expressions of support for IS to mean official pledges of allegiance to al-Baghdadi[76]. In October 2014, more TTP leaders bolted and apparently pledged allegiance to al-Baghdadi, which raised more loyalty questions[77]. By January 2015, pledges of allegiance to IS by mid-level TTP commanders and officials materialized in a video analyzed by *The Long War Journal*[78]. The video, released on 10 January, but likely produced in October 2014[79], featured a number of Pakistani Taliban commanders and officials pledging new allegiance, and reiterating previous pledges of allegiance, to IS and al-Baghdadi. A digest of notable mentions follows: (1) Speaking on behalf of the **recently formed Khorasan Media group** that released the video was former TTP spokesman Sheikh Maqbool aka Shahid Shahidullah. Maqbool introduced Hafiz Saeed Khan as **overall emir of the Khorasan Shura**[80] **consultation council.** Khan previously served as the TTP's emir for the tribal agency of Arakzai, Pakistan. Maqbool also claimed that consent to nominate Khan as emir came from several jihadists from Kabul and Kunduz, Afghanistan who were unable to attend the shura meeting. The shura council reportedly consists of mostly low to mid-level former TTP militants. (2) (A) **New IS pledges** by those reportedly appearing in person on the video came from the following areas: (a) Logar and Kunar, Afghanistan (b) Islamabad, Peshawar, and Lakki Marwat, Pakistan (c) The AfPak region via Jawad, pledging new allegiance to IS and representing **Abtalul Islam** (Heroes of Islam) **Foundation, a jihadi media group** that pledged allegiance to IS in July 2014. (B) Representation under the new pledge category from Pakistan included a TTP faction called the Sa'ad bin Abi Waqas Front that emerged in Logar, Afghanistan. (3) **Previous pledges to IS that were reiterated in the video** came from representatives from the following areas: (a) Hangu, Peshawar, Kurram, and Khyber, Pakistan. (4) **Claims of IS pledges that could not be delivered in person** at the shura council, according to Maqbool, came from the following areas: (a) Kunar and Nagarhar, Afghanistan (b) Khyber Agency, Bajaur Agency, Dir, and Waziristan, Pakistan.

The IS-aligned media groups, the recently formed Khorasan Shura and its emerging emir, and the pledges emanating from Afghanistan and Pakistan indicate that IS is not only gaining support, but also building an infrastructure in South and Central Asia, where AQ has traditionally maintained a presence. Further underscoring the IS endeavor in this region, an audio taped speech released on 26 January 2015 titled, "Say, Die in Your Rage!" featured IS spokesman Abu Muhammad al Adnani announcing IS expansion into

"Khorasan," lands which include modern-day Afghanistan and Pakistan and portions of other countries in close proximity; and the announcement of two appointments: (1) former TTP commander Hafez Saeed Khan as "governor" of the Khorasan province, and (2) Mullah Adbul Rauf Khadim, reportedly a former senior Taliban commander in southern Afghanistan, as "deputy governor [81]." He is likely the same aforementioned Mullah Abdul Rauf who is an ex-Guantanamo detainee[37]. The IS undertaking in this region is unfolding on the heels of the formal end of U.S. and NATO combat operations in December 2014 in Afghanistan. As such, IS is testing the waters to see where it could best exploit under-governed areas experiencing gaps in security. Also, the IS continues to bring disaffected TTP cadres into its fold, and they are surfacing in Afghanistan. U.S. Intelligence officials told *The Long War Journal* that TTP lost more than 70 percent of its strength during the split[82].

> "The Taliban seek to topple the
> Pakistan Government, impose Shariah,
> seize Pakistani nuclear weapons and
> wage jihad until the Caliphate is
> established across the world."

Still another notable development: The TTP split gave rise to Jamaat-ul-Ahrar TTP (JuA)[83] in August 2014, which vowed to "continue armed struggle for the enforcement of Islamic Sharia[84]" to fulfill the parent TTP's original objective of forming an Islamic state[85]. The JuA merged with TTP faction Ahrar-ul-Hind and brought in the powerful TTP chapter chief of the Mohmand Agency, Abdul Wali alias Omar Khalid al-Khorasani, a close associate of AQC's al-Zawahiri. On 20 March 2012, Wali succinctly laid out the parent TTP's game plan, which, per JuA's vow, would carry over to this merger:

A Closer Look at Nuclear-Armed Pakistan

Pakistan's nuclear sites are thought to be located in the north and west, in areas populated by Taliban and AQ supporters[86]. The country has suffered several terrorist attacks on its nuclear facilities and associated personnel since 2003[87]. Pakistan's generals control the nuclear weapons, some of which are mobilized. The generals reportedly expressed concern that their Prime Minister, Nawaz Sharif, wants to bring Pakistan's Taliban into a coalition government in his own drive to become emir of a caliphate[88]. The top brass is also worried that a Taliban-ruled Afghanistan would employ jihad to merge native Pashtuns in Pakistan and in Afghanistan per an old Afghan plan for the Pashtunistan region spanning both countries, including reaching into Pakistan's sensitive north and west. Concerns over the military itself, and over Pakistan's ISI also linger: Military personnel may be influenced by jihadist sympathies, despite a supposed post-9-11 purging of jihad supporters from its ranks[89]. An Islamic coup d'état could occur, either by the military, particularly the 10 Corps that guards the Kahuta nuclear weapons complex in Punjab Province, the Army General Headquarters, and the government's seat of power in Islamabad; or by the ISI, some of whose civilian and military personnel provide freelance support for Islamic militants[90]. There are also mounting concerns that Pakistan and India, another nuclear-armed state, could slide into full-scale war, [91] which could include a cyber war dimension, over reported provocations by the Pakistan Army[92].

Al-Zawahiri is likely using Pakistan as a safe haven[93]. If so, he is well-positioned to tap key participants in the terrorist syndicate to help advance his caliphate project if he weathers the IS challenge and the rift within his network[94]. Pakistan's worsening fragility would facilitate al-Zawahiri's endeavors: The Fragile State Index (FSI) informs that this country tumbled from #13 in 2013 to #10 in 2014, with the #1 slot representing the least stable state[95]. Another facilitating factor may be U.S. and NATO partners ending their combat mission in Afghanistan – #7 in the 2014 FSI. Despite the planned reduction in counter-terrorism activity expected during Operation Resolute Support in 2015[96], the Taliban and AQ are likely to antagonize the multi-national troops back into the fight.

According to a 13 August 2014 assessment by Col. HPD Hansi, senior fellow at the Centre for Land Warfare Studies in New Delhi: **"NATO has failed in weakening the Taliban[97]."** The capacity of State Police mechanism to deal with terrorists "remains doubtful," he said, and informed of three major security problems challenging Pakistan today: sectarianism, which is deteriorating; the rapidly changing demography of Karachi[98] due to a very large influx of Pashtuns, and a sharp decline of Mohajirs, such that there is "a huge conflict brewing in the city;" and "Talibanisation," whereby the Taliban raised the level of violence and broadened its scope in a number of areas, and it threatens to spread the violence further. He said that news reports alleging that Taliban leaders enjoy safe haven in Pakistani army camps in Kurram, coupled with no major TTP leader being killed so far "… raises serious questions on the Army's stance regarding Taliban." Pakistan's support of the Afghan Taliban "continues unabated," he said, noting "ambiguity about the role of the army towards the radical outfits," which translates into "whether the Army will continue supporting these non-state actors using the Islamic crutch to further their agenda."

In order to realize his vision, the deeply networked al-Zawahiri would have to prod the reclusive Omar into laying claim to an authoritative caliphate without delay and into expanding the Afghan Taliban's regional horizons. If al-Zawahiri succeeds, he could bring renewed relevance to AQC and save face in the contest with al-Baghdadi, whose enterprise is awash in military successes, money streams[99] and foreign fighters honing their combat skills in a prime theatre for subsequent ops back home. If Omar does not rise to the occasion to offer a robust counter to the IS caliphate project, pressure will continue to mount within the jihadi world for AQC and IS to reconcile. If al-Zawahiri refuses, he will become increasingly isolated from his network as al-Baghdadi continues plundering under infidel fire, resultantly growing in influence, power, wealth, territory, and followers eager for booty and position. If an alliance does emerge between these two leaders and their respective entities and enterprises, it likely will be tactical, full of intrigue, and terrifying for some period of time due to increased operational effectiveness, but it will not endure.

The Gory-to-Glory Argument Gaining Traction

In a broader sense, the IS declaration of a caliphate perched atop growing heaps of corpses, captured booty, and conquered territories has given fresh impetus to the long-running argument in the Islamic world – based upon the Qur'an and the Sunna – that jihad, rather than the democratic process, is the way forward to usher the ummah into an unprecedented chapter of Islamic glory. The gory-to-glory argument is buoyed by the letdown of the Arab Spring, which failed to advance Muslim aspirations for a global caliphate via the democratic process.

With the intoxicating allure of the thus far successful albeit savage IS enterprise, and the justification for violent jihad gaining traction worldwide, jihadists are striving with renewed fervor to carve out their own spheres of influence to ensure their places among the power elite that they expect to arise from the most durable caliphate, which would bind together the Islamic nodes dotting the globe to create their anticipated New World Order.

FOCUS ON AFRICA

Hizb-ut Tahrir: Clandestine Course to a Revived Caliphate

Hizb-ut Tahrir (HT), or Party of Liberation, is taking advantage of Pakistan's high level of instability and is making it a priority via its secretive cells there to establish a caliphate per the Muhammadan tradition[100]. This global Salafist political party's objectives for Pakistan is tellingly laid out in a 2011 monograph entitled, "Return of the Khilafa[101]: A Vision of Pakistan Under the Khilafa and How an Islamic Constitution Will Give Rise to Policies of Revival." The militant group plans to take the reins of power ostensibly via a bloodless military coup d'état – a recurrent event in Pakistan. Toward this end, the HT in Pakistan has been recruiting top brass and key civil officers; indoctrinating youth at prominent universities; implementing a media campaign targeting the populace with workshops, seminars, and free distribution of publications, CDs, and open letters; and disseminating letters and video messages urging military chiefs to take action on behalf of the Muslim world.

The HT has a three-stage strategy[102]: (1) recruit and agitate people to adopt the party line in order to form party groups or cells; (2) interact with the ummah for the purpose of Islamization; (3) establish government by implementing Islam generally and comprehensively until the party base is strong enough and the conditions are right for a revolutionary takeover of the existing governing structure via jihad. The party's founder, sheikh Taqiuddin an-Nabhani al Falastini, drafted a constitution and reportedly wrote that the religious imperative upon the ummah to revive the caliphate is so strong that Mohammad's close companions delayed burying his body until a caliph was appointed and the caliphate was established. An-Nabhani's anticipated caliph would appoint an emir, a military leader who would declare jihad and wage war against all non-Muslim peoples. Toward that end, the HT is a proponent of a strong Islamic army capable of aggressively expanding the caliphate's boundaries via offensive jihad in order to overthrow established political regimes and wage war on the West, with America specifically in its crosshairs.

Like the HT, other Muslim entities are building shadow or parallel systems of governance designed to undermine and eventually supplant existing state apparatuses either when they have strong enough bases of power or upon the establishment of the anticipated global caliphate. This pattern holds true not only in Asia and Africa, but also in the diaspora. For instance: Among Sunni entities, the transcontinental Muslim Brotherhood, to which An-Nabhani once belonged and which has spawned numerous Muslim terrorist organizations, devised and is implementing a phased strategic plan, broad in scope, that leverages Western freedoms and tolerance to prep the ground in North America for a global caliphate[103]. Among Shi'ite entities, the Shia Imami Ismaili Muslims are subject to a global constitution, which their jet-setting "Imam of the Atomic Age," Prince Karim Al Husseini Aga Khan – who claims to be a direct descendant of Muhammad, and who owns a university in Pakistan – ordained to supersede the constitutions of the countries hosting his flock, with the palliative stipulation that his document is subject only to the overriding effect of any law of the land[104]. The fruit of this widespread Islamic strategy to implement, and eventually enforce, sharia in countries hosting Muslim diaspora communities can be seen manifesting in regions that include Europe and North America, with the United Kingdom, the U.S., and Canada as particular targets.

Taken as a whole, Islamic entities, including cultural centers, religious establishments, educational institutions, youth clubs, professional organizations, for-profits, NGOs, charities, banks, *hawalas*[105], legal bodies, security committees, and political parties, are propagating Islam and promoting the seemingly benign *da'wa*[106] in every strata of their host societies in preparation for melding into the power infrastructure of their anticipated global caliphate: a muted process until Islam's determined advance meets resistance. Islam inculcates in its adherents that resistance to the advancement of the religion is oppression, which opens the door for "defensive" jihad once capabilities are in place. In a collective quest to advance the religion, these Islamic entities make up a vast global infrastructure of legitimate, quasi-legitimate, and illegitimate institutions and organizations that work together synergistically alongside Muslim states, and non-Muslim stakeholders, to not only promote *da'wa*, but to directly and indirectly serve as a resource provider, facilitator, and cover for jihad – all with the goal of reviving the caliphate, and much of which undermines the existing global order.

Boko Haram: Stakes Savage Claim to a Caliphate in Nigeria

The heavily armed, well-funded, Nigerian-rooted Boko Haram laid claim to a self-styled caliphate via a video released in August 2014[107]. Boko Haram's feared fundamentalist leader, Abu Muhammad Abubaker bin Muhammad Shekau, announced in the video that the predominantly Christian town of Gwoza was part of "the Islamic caliphate," but did not specify if his caliphate was linked to the professed IS caliphate or if it was independent[108]. Shekau's group seized Gwoza in early August after his operatives were alleged to have killed more than 100 civilians. An October 2014 video using the IS flag and music during a similar declaration by Shekau concerning dozens of local government areas that fell under Boko Haram's brutal control indicates identification with the IS project, and opens the possibility that he may link his project to the IS caliphate[109].

Boko Haram continues with impunity to seize key territories to the detriment of the populations therein[110] per its plans to expand its caliphate throughout greater West Africa. With increasing ferocity, this group is executing large-scale attacks on civilians, particularly targeting Christians[111], while also killing others, including Muslims[112]. Spokesman for the northern group of the Christian Association of Nigeria on 6 December 2012[113] decried the continued attacks on Christians; an issue he said was not getting enough government attention.

"What people get to hear is just a fraction of the attacks Christian are subjected to," he said, adding, "It is unfortunate that when the (Christian Association of Nigeria) president comments on the issue, they accuse him of not being sensitive or raising false alarm."

WorldWatch Monitor, "10 Killed, Four Churches Burned in Nigeria"

According to Raymond Ibrahim, who authors the monthly Gatestone Institute report, "Muslim Persecution of Christians," which has been chronicling attacks on Christians in dozens of countries since 2011, in just four years, Boko Haram has destroyed around 1,000 churches, which has made Nigeria one of the most dangerous places for Christians[114]. Ibrahim noted that although Muslim-on-

Muslim violence captures headlines, media coverage of Muslim violence against Christians goes underreported, and political awareness of the problem is lacking.

In what the human rights organization Amnesty International said could be Boko Haram's deadliest attack, beginning on 3 January 2015, operatives launched a raid and seized the town of Baga, as well as 16 neighboring villages, where they indiscriminately slaughtered hundreds and possibly up to 2,000 civilians, and displaced at least 30,000[115]. Daniel Eyre, Nigeria researcher for Amnesty International, said if reports are true that the town was razed and the civilian death toll rose to hundreds or even up to 2000, then this outrage "marks a disturbing and bloody escalation of Boko Haram's ongoing onslaught against the civilian population." Standing on evidence it has gathered, Amnesty International informed that Boko Haram members have committed war crimes and crimes against humanity, and noted that since 2009, the terrorist group has deliberately targeted civilians, launching raids and bomb attacks with increasing frequency and severity.

Defense experts assess that this group is close to attaining its goal of controlling a large, economically self-sustaining area across northern Nigeria due to failure of the Nigerian military to stop the insurgency[116]. On 25 January 2015, the group launched an attack on Maiduguri, the capital of Borno State, and engaged government troops in fierce fighting, and launched a simultaneous attack on the strategic buffer town of Monguno, putting troops to flight, seizing the military barracks, and taking control of an urban area with a population of about 100,000[117]. If Shekau holds the large swathes of territory his group seized in mainly north and northeastern Nigeria during the latter half of 2014, especially in Borno State[118], he may deem his caliphate durable enough to be independent – perhaps provisionally – from other emerging or evolving Islamic entities. In the 19th century, the Sokoto caliphate and its notable slave society spanned an area that included what are now Nigeria, Niger, and Cameroon, and it was regarded as independent from other Muslim empires[119]. In keeping with this area's Islamic history, Boko Haram prospers from the slave trade[120] and operates in all three of these countries[121]. In the first admission that Boko Haram has been operating in Cameroon, Shekau warned Cameroonian President Paul Biya in a YouTube video posted on 5 January 2015 that Cameroon would meet the same fate as that which is befalling Nigeria[122].

Shekau is rigorously building a reputation as a ruthless and uncompromising jihadi leader capable of conquering and holding territory and enforcing sharia in a region that was once part of a "glorious" Islamic empire. Consequently, at least for now, he appears to have several options at his disposal:

formally committing to the IS caliphate project at its outset; remaining independent if he becomes strong enough; or tying in with the most durable caliphate, be it the IS or the AQ caliphate or some other caliphate formation, should such an entity become firmly established in the region and acknowledged by the Muslim world.

Shekau is also aspiring to raise his group's profile as Nigeria's wing in the transnational jihadi-sphere[123]. A July 2014 video release shows him voicing support for IS, Taliban, and AQ leaders[124]. Boko Haram draws inspiration from the Taliban[125], and refers to itself as the "Nigerian Taliban[126]." Shekau also has been voicing support for AQ since he became leader of Boko Haram in July 2010, but he has fallen short of formally pledging allegiance to al-Zawahiri. Boko Haram maintains ties with AQIM, which is working to topple perceived apostate African regimes[127], to expand into the Sahel, and to re-conquer the Iberian Peninsula[128]. AQIM has provided material support and training to Boko Haram, including giving instructions on how to construct improvised explosive devices, which notably strengthened the latter's operational capabilities in Africa[129]. In a March 2014 video translated from Hausa, Shekau reportedly affirmed Boko Haram's "African struggle[130]." While not abandoning the local struggle, Shekau supports AQ's global vision, and backs this support with attacks on Westerners in the region, and with promises to launch attacks against the West once his capabilities enable him to make good on his threats[131]. In a December 2013 videotaped speech in Arabic, Hausa, and Kanuri, Shekau reportedly warned that Boko Haram's operations would not be confined to Nigeria and he promised that the U.S. would see his operatives in its homeland[132]. Shekau must be careful to strike a balance within his breakaway faction[133] if he is to satisfy the locally driven motivations of his followers while advancing AQ's global vision.

Relevantly, in the August 2014 video, a high-spirited Shekau trumpeted: **"Allah commands us to rule Gwoza by Islamic law. In fact, he commands us to rule the rest of the world, not only in Nigeria, and now we have started[134]."** Shekau is known for his uncompromising stance on the interpretation of the Qur'an and *Ahadith*[135], the latter of which records the traditions, examples, sayings, and approvals of Muhammad. Shekau officially named his faction the Sunni Community Committed to the Propagation of the Prophet's Teachings and Jihad or *Jama'atu Ahlis Sunna Lidda'awati wal-Jihad*[136]. Boko Haram draws inspiration from an excerpt from Qur'an 5:47, which reads: **"And whoever does not judge by what Allah has sent down, so those are the transgressors[137]."** There is ample instructive material in the Qur'an and in *Ahadith* regarding how Muslims are to judge and to punish "transgressors" of Allah's sharia as his followers strive to establish a global caliphate and to build an Islamic New World Order from which to rule over non-Muslims. Terrorist attacks in the service of jihad perpetrated by Boko Haram and by other Muslim terrorist groups are, indeed, the fruit of faithful adherence to Qur'anic texts. Informed Boko Haram in a video reportedly released at the end of December 2014 featuring the execution of civilians the group deemed "infidels" in a dormitory: **"We have made sure the floor of this hall is turned red with blood, and this is how it is going to be in all future attacks and arrests of infidels. From now (on), killing, slaughtering, destructions and bombing will be our religious duty anywhere we invade.**[138]**"**

Ansar al-Sharias of Benghazi and Derna Forge Emirates; in Derna, an IS Province

On 30 July 2014, Ansar al-Sharia in Libya[139] (ASL) declared Benghazi an Islamic emirate after claiming it seized complete control of this northeastern port city[140], which is a hub serving sea and land pipelines for smuggling weapons and militants to destinations in the Sinai, Gaza, and Syria[141]. Responding to the announcement, which aired on *Radio Tawhid*, retired army general Khalifa Haftar, who heads a private army that is trying to rid Benghazi of Islamic militants, denied ASL's claim, and said his forces only made a "tactical withdrawal[142]" from the city. Libya's Ansar al-Sharia movement belongs to the Muslim Brotherhood-affiliated Shura Council[143] of Benghazi Revolutionaries, a powerful alliance of militias[144] with elements complicit in or otherwise linked to the 11 September 2012 attack on the U.S. Special Mission and Annex in Benghazi[145]. Since mid-July, this shura has been on an armed offensive involving the seizure of several military bases in the Benghazi region, including the Special Forces camp, where the alliance commandeered large quantities of arms, rockets, ammunition, and armored vehicles. Logistical help from ASL is provided to fighters in Benghazi training camps and elsewhere in eastern Libya [146]; additionally, ASL works with local businesses, organizations, and education institutions to provide community services to the populace in order to win goodwill, firm up its grip on power, and enforce sharia[147].

The U.S. State Department treats the Libya-based Ansar al-Sharia Derna (ASD) as a separate terrorist group from its ASL parent, but acknowledged both were involved in the 11 Sep 2012 Benghazi attack[148], which the Obama administration misleadingly blamed on a film that depicted the Islamic prophet, Muhammad, in an unfavorable light. The ASD aims to build an Islamic state[149]. The port city of Derna is a strategic Salafist stronghold along the aforementioned smuggling pipelines, and is a safe haven for foreign jihadi groups and local militias. Militias in Libya cooperate with ASD and make up much of AQ's network in this country[150]. There are other ASL branches based in Libya, as well[151].

A merger comprising ASD, the Islamic State Army, and supporters of Abu Sufian bin Qumu[152], a former Guantanamo detainee, resulted in the March 2014 formation of the heavily armed *Majlis Shura Shabab Al-Islam* (MSSI) or Shura Council of Islamist Youth, which declared Derna an Islamic emirate[153]. In early October, the MSSI dubbed its seized territory in Derna a *wilayat* or province of the IS caliphate project, to which it pledged allegiance[154]; and in November, its oath of allegiance was accepted by al-Baghdadi[155]. To ensure implementation of sharia law, the MSSI formed a de facto legal committee parallel to the Libyan government's official legal institution. Copying IS, the MSSI called for perceived Muslim apostates to repent, warned that Jews and Christians who refuse to convert to Islam will be targeted, and deployed patrols at the city's entrances to enforce its will[156]. Notably, the MSSI controls al-Huraysh Hospital in Derna[157], which can double as a command center and an infirmary for wounded jihadists, while denying care to opponents. The Pentagon in early December publicly expressed concerns that IS had established a base of operation in the country, with the terrorist entity running training camps in Derna, and reportedly dispensing executions and floggings in the city[158]. The MSSI and other groups striving to establish sharia-compliant legal systems to usurp existing legal systems within their respective countries thrive in part because they exploit deficiencies in governmental capacity, the lack of political will to push back, uncoordinated international counter-terrorism efforts, and an atmosphere of domestic tolerance and fear. The ASD plans to expand this emirate-turned-province to Benghazi[159]. Tactical coordination between ASD and ASL exists[160]; but the relationship between their claimed emirates is as yet unclear. Libyan security officials believe that the MSSI is behind a wave of assassinations targeting police and judges.

Tunisian security officials believe operational, financial, and logistical ties exist between Ansar al-Sharia in Tunisia (AST) and ASL with the latter reportedly equipping the former with weapons[161]. Both groups missionize at home and send jihadists abroad, including to Syria[162].

Generally speaking: Since 2012, the Ansar al-Sharia movement has been advancing from da'wa to violent jihad: a common tendency among jihadist groups given that the two strategies to propagate Islam have historically gone hand-in-hand. Although the most prominent Ansar al-Sharia groups are the ones in Yemen, Libya, and Tunisia, newer groups recently have formed in Egypt and Morocco. These groups have become part of the post-Arab Spring Salafia Jihadia upsurge in Asia and Africa[163]. Ansar al-Sharia groups are waging jihad to impose a Talban-style caliphate system. Although the Ansar al-Sharia groups share a similar name and ideology, they lack a unified command structure[164], which could hamper strategic and operational effectiveness. Unifying these groups and their projects into one caliphate system would mitigate this problem, and apparently this is the direction the Ansar al-Sharia movement is heading. Although the Ansar al-Sharia groups have served as "the ideological face, the human reservoir and money provider for the armed AQ[165]," and many of them have declared loyalty to AQC, the groups in Libya and in Tunisia favor strong ties with IS, and the group in Yemen supported IS even before al-Baghdadi declared a caliphate[166]. Ansar al-Sharia groups in Libya and in Tunisia, along with other top jihadi organizations in North Africa, have been considering unification of some groups in the area, particularly those in Libya, Tunisia, Algeria, and Mali and have been ruminating on the idea of establishing an Islamic state in the Islamic Maghreb to be allied with IS[167]. Barring an effective pre-emptive counter-measure from AQC, which has formal affiliates in the area that could act as spoilers, unification of top groups and an alliance that combines their respective projects and that favors IS could further empower al-Baghdadi and give his caliphate project a foothold in northern Africa, if such an arrangement proves durable. Moreover, a durable arrangement could facilitate extending the IS caliphate project southward because of the strong regional associations that would be inherent in the unified entity brought into the alliance.

Operation Dawn Coalition Sets Up De Facto Islamic Government in Tripoli

After candidates sympathetic to jihadist causes[168] suffered significant losses in Libya's Council of Representatives parliamentary elections on 25 June 2014[169], the Operation Dawn Coalition aka Fajr Libya of Islamic militias, and revolutionary Muslim Brotherhood-linked Misrata Brigades, conducted a five-week siege of Tripoli[170]; snatched the Tripoli International Airport on 23 August from rival Zintan Brigades[171], a marginally pro-government militia[172] guarding the site, and then defiantly proclaimed a new government[173]. Contrary to legal procedure, the outgoing jihadist-supporting parliament, the General National Congress, unilaterally reconvened on 25 August in Tripoli, declared that it replaced the Council of Representatives, Libya's official government, and elected jihadist-backed Omar al-Hassani as prime minister[174]. Consequently, the de facto government is seated in Libya's capital and chief port city, Tripoli, comprising commercial, financial, aviation, and seaport hubs[175] in the predominantly tribal west, while the official government, at least on paper, meets in the restive east, docked offshore at the Tobruq port[176]. East Libya is home to 60 percent of Libya's oil production[177], and haven for local militias and an increasing number of foreign jihadists.

The bloody geo-political contest, and the two rival governments and parliaments – in typical Islamic brinksmanship fashion – are inching Libya ever closer to failed state status[178] as the dramatic power play runs its course on domestic turf that is also home to Africa's largest proven crude oil reserves[179].

Libya's fledgling Council of Representatives has deemed the Operation Dawn Coalition a terrorist organization[180]. After the authoritative *Small Arms Survey*[181] conducted field research in Misrata in March 2012, it reported that following the 2011 revolt against Muammar Qaddafi's regime, the Misrata Brigades controlled about 75-85 percent of Libya's non-state combatants and weapons stockpiles[182]. Many of the weapons, including anti-tank guided weapons and man-portable air-defense systems, remain in brigade inventories.

The revolutionary militias and transnational jihadist groups continue to rapidly gain significant geo-strategic ground and self-professed authority in Libya. If this situation continues, resource-rich Libya could devolve into a self-sustaining Islamic terrorist state fully plugged into the regional network of fortifying Islamic terrorist entities, thus contributing to further instability in Africa and Asia, and by extension, significantly elevating the global threat environment.

Al-Shabaab Insurgent Group in Somalia Striving for Islamic Emirate

Al-Shabaab is the largest insurgent group fighting the Somali government, with the former determined to supplant the latter with a Salafist emirate[183]. In January 2010, this hybrid terrorist organization[184] also called for combining jihad in Horn of Africa with global jihad via the AQ network[185]. Despite resulting fissures in its leadership caused in part by "glocalizing[186]" its local fight [187], Al-Shabaab portrays itself as engaged in a global battle against non-Muslims, and calls for the reunification of the ummah in the struggle for a global Islamic state[188].

In February 2012, the group pledged allegiance to al-Zawahiri, who announced that Al-Shabaab joined AQ[189]. After the formal merger, al-Zawahiri said he envisioned Somalia as the fortress of Islam and jihad in East Africa. In September 2014, Al-Shabaab used the occasion of the targeted killing of its feared co-founder and emir, Ahmed Abdi Aw-Mohamed aka Godane, to not only announce its new emir, Ahmad Umar aka Abu Ubaidah[190], but to also renew the group's pledge of allegiance to AQ and al-Zawahiri, and to reaffirm Taliban leader Omar as "commander of the faithful[191]." Al-Shabaab's principles are modeled after those of the Taliban[192].

At an October 2014 counter-piracy conference in Dubai, however, United Arab Emirates foreign minister, Sheik Abdullah bin Zayed Al Nahyan, said that Al-Shabaab may be collaborating with IS, and while he did not cite specific intelligence, he did warn that more should be done to prepare for such an eventuality[193]. There has been some speculation that Al-Shabaab may shift its allegiance from AQ to IS[194] because now months into his new leadership role, Ahmad Umar has kept silent about his group's renewed pledge to AQ and to al-Zawahiri[195]. Little is known about Ahmad Umar, even within Al-Shabaab, but he is said to have joined the group between 1997 and 2006, and to have been close to his predecessor, Aw-Mohamed.

The United Nations (UN) Monitoring Group on Somalia and Eritrea in its latest annual report in October 2014 warned that Al-Shabaab "remains the principal threat to peace and security in Somalia and throughout the Horn of Africa[196]." Moreover, the monitoring group noted that targeted airstrikes netted short-term gains, yet significantly failed to diminish the terrorist group's operational capacity, and that foreign counter-terrorism operations furthered Al-Shabaab's propaganda efforts[197]." The monitoring group also documented large-scale, systematic diversion of arms and ammunition taken from Somali National Army (SNA) stockpiles and directly transferred to the black market in Mogadishu by high-level corrupt Somali officials from this internationally backed government; and these illicit arms are then purchased by Al-Shabaab agents.

Despite a crackdown against the group since 2011, whereby the African Union Mission in Somalia (AMISOM) and, to a lesser extent, Somali forces, have been pushing Al-Shabaab out of Somalia's major cities and strongholds, the insurgent group still controls large sections of rural areas throughout the south and central areas of the country, including territories in the Bay, Shabelle, and Bokool regions, and in the middle and lower Juba region, from where the terrorist group launches large-scale attacks targeting Mogadishu[198]. The monitoring group informed that Al-Shabaab enhanced its capacity by maintaining an effective and violent footprint in Somalia's capital while tactically withdrawing from certain territories[199]. Al-Shabaab also is using Somalia's long, unguarded coastline to good effect[200].

Al-Shabaab's operations were significantly degraded by Operation Indian Ocean[201], a renewed offensive by AMISOM forces and the SNA, resulting in the terrorist group losing towns in south and central Somalia, including two along the eastern coastline: the key port town, Barawe[202], and the trading coastal town,

Cadale[203]. The monitoring group informed that AMISOM faces "serious challenges" to stabilizing recovered locations, however, because Al-Shabaab withdraws from these areas and then counter-attacks with regular, even "complex," asymmetrical operations[204]; demonstrating its ability to endure kinetic counter-terrorism campaigns despite having emerged from a fractious state. Moreover, on 8 November 2014, the group launched what security sources have determined was Al-Shabaab's largest conventional assault since its emir, Aw-Mohamed, was killed[205]. The major offensive, which resulted in heavy casualties, targeted the strategic Kudha Island that was reportedly recently seized by local, Kenyan, and AMISOM forces. The island, 40 miles from the key port and former Al-Shabaab stronghold of Kismayo, is a major staging post of illegal charcoal exports, an important revenue source for this terrorist group.

In anticipation of a renewed counter-terrorism offensive in south and central regions of the Somalia, Al-Shabaab augmented its presence in the northern region, mainly in Puntland[206], and is deftly utilizing the northern coastline. Al-Shabaab expanded into Puntland's larger urban centers; increased its presence and movement in the regions of Bari, Mudug, and Nugaal[207]; and concentrated its forces within the accommodating Golis Mountain Range, which extends from the border with Ethiopia to Cape Guardafui[208]. From these areas, Al-Shabaab operatives have conducted large-scale military operations in the vicinity[209]. In 2012, Al-Shabaab merged with the Galgala militia[210], and for several years held Galgala, a gateway town to the Golis Mountain Range; however, the terrorist group and Puntland's de facto authorities both claimed control of the area after recent clashing[211]. The monitoring group alleges that Puntland de facto president Abdiweli Mohamed Ali Gaas is protecting Al-Shabaab, hindering investigations, implementing a "catch and release" policy of its operatives, and abetting its regional activities.

The terrorist group is also under investigation for renewed infiltration into the Sool region of nearby (British) Somaliland in the northwest, where it was caught recruiting[212].

Al-Shabaab's presence in northern Somalia enables it to work closely with AQAP, an official AQ affiliate, which in 2011 declared Yemen's southern Abyan Province an Islamic emirate and since September 2014 has executed attacks in nearly half of this country's 21 provinces[213]. Al-Shabaab trains in AQAP camps in Yemen, where these two groups fight the Yemeni army, and Al-Shabaab militants return to Somalia with honed combat skills and bomb-making expertise for use in operations in Africa[214]. From Somalia's northern coastline, these two groups coordinate the movement of weapons, fighters, and supplies between Yemen and Somalia; AQAP also maintains a presence in Puntland, including within the Golis Mountain Range[215].

A resourceful insurgent group, Al-Shabaab has a strong media presence[216] like other key Islamic terrorist groups, but unlike most of these groups, it has previous governing experience, particularly in Somalia. The group is also engaged in a diverse range of illicit activities and is well networked. Tapping a cross-section of Somali clans and sub-clans, Al-Shabaab's leadership established a basic insurgent sharia-based Islamic government that functioned as an alternative to the weak post-civil war interim national governments during the height of the group's territorial and administrative expansion in Somalia from 2008 to 2010[217]. This terrorist group adeptly leverages clan rivalries for political advantage; its diverse fiscal base[218] adequately funds its jihad operations; it is engaged in da'wa activities and in social services to reinvigorate support from local communities[219]; and it teaches potential Somali recruits their ethnic, religious, and historical identities to incite them into action against the West[220]. Al-Shabaab is also piped into an entrenched and elastic regional network of non-state, anti-Western actors, involving expatriate Somali communities, refugees in UN camps, affiliates, pirate leaders, and illegal fishers. All of these are connections that bolster its intelligence gathering and staging abilities, operational reach, supplies lines, and recruitment and financing activities[221].

The politically astute, highly adaptable, resurgent Al-Shabaab is demonstrating in no uncertain terms that it is still a force to be reckoned with, despite its fractured leadership, the loss of some local support, the recent loss of its co-founder, and its retreat from some territories.

This group can be expected to continue exploiting Somalia's weak and corrupt central government, as well as AMISOM's lack of maritime and aviation assets, and armored personnel carriers[222]. The restructured and more militant[223] Al-Shabaab is involved in a sustained campaign of increasingly lethal attacks throughout southern and central Somalia, and it is inspiring and coordinating noteworthy attacks against neighboring countries[224]; such asymmetrical operations will likely continue. Recent setbacks for Al-Shabaab serve as lessons learned. Accordingly, this group can be expected to continue adjusting its tactics and strategies[225] to more effectively respond to its fluid and hostile operational environment[226].

Al-Shabaab's relationship with the AQ network, and particularly with AQAP, serves as a force and capability multiplier. Providing its loyalties remain with AQ, Al-Shabaab will continue tapping this key resource to facilitate operations aimed at recovering lost ground and making headway into new territories, and it will likely become more involved in AQ operations beyond Yemen.

If, however, Ahmad Umar shifts allegiance to IS, then more fracturing within Al-Shabaab is likely to occur. If such an alliance proves durable, it would significantly increase the threat that IS poses to Asia and Africa, to international shipping routes and commerce, and to the West in general. Sunni and Shi'a tensions would be palpable. Iran would respond to the growing IS threat by bolstering its influence particularly in Saudi Arabia's Eastern Province, Bahrain, and Yemen, and it would see the development as further reason to fast-track its nuclear weapons program.

Like many other jihadist groups, Al-Shabaab will become further emboldened and further energized by an evolving caliphate – regardless of which terrorist organization has the wherewithal to bring this core Islamic institution into full-blooded realization. The group can thus be expected to soldier on, come what may, toward establishing its Salafist emirate.

Other factors contributing to the rise of a caliphate

Despite the best counter-terrorism efforts, conditions in the regional atmosphere are conducive to the institution of a durable caliphate for an unknown period of time.

Asia and Africa are beset by weak and corrupt governments whose authorities are undermined by well-heeled[227], social service-providing Muslim terrorist groups leveraging their respective state's lack of capacity and governmental legitimacy. Such social programs are used by the terrorist groups to win the hearts and minds of the locals and other targeted audiences; to indoctrinate the needy to garner their assistance; and to create an air of respectability in the international community in order to build up popular bases of support and to frustrate the issuance of terrorist designations.

The region's rivaling tribes and burgeoning youth populations[228] are schooled at all levels in generations-old anti-Western Islamic narratives crowned with rousing topics like ending the aforementioned Sykes-Picot Agreement, which in 1916, in the interest of introducing order, expediently established a nation-state system that lacked regard for tribal divisions. Such narratives are juxtaposed with revisionist teachings that obfuscate the long legacy of Muhammad-inspired jihadi conquests and colonization targeting Western civilizations, and other "infidel" communities – including those within the region – since the inception of Islam, which is glorified by a steady diet of slick propaganda.

In step with rising self-determination and eroding state sovereignty, Asia and Africa are experiencing proliferating post-Arab-Spring sectarianism. The Arab Spring's failure to deliver a caliphate via peaceful democratic means also led to the Salafia Jihadia movement gaining significant traction in the region. Resultantly, Islamic unions, youth groups, and other Muslim organizations are growing more militant[229] – a trend that will rise regionally and globally, and that will affect individual Muslims as the West continues its efforts to mitigate the growing Islamic terrorist threat emanating from Asia and Africa.

An increasing number of under-governed spaces like the Sinai Peninsula, and ungoverned spaces like the "Salvador Triangle" straddling the borders of Libya, Algeria, and Niger, are providing safe havens for jihadists, smugglers, and traffickers; and are serving as jihadi training zones, and staging grounds for terrorist attacks targeting regional and Western interests. Islamic terrorist groups, fronts, and alliances are successfully fortifying their operations via seizures of strategic assets, including military bases, oil fields, waterways, key ports, and main roads.

It is not lost on Iran that it is in the crosshairs of the growing regional Sunni threat, which will only escalate if a nuclear-armed Sunni Pakistan falls into terrorist hands – a likely scenario[230]. Add to this al-Baghdadi's caliphate announcement that pejoratively applied the term *rafidah*[231] to the Shi'ites and rolled them into the IS category of targets[232] in hopes of rallying Sunni support. Despite claims otherwise, Iran can be expected to continue on its trajectory toward achieving a deliverable nuclear weapons capability[233]. Moreover, Iran's expanding hegemony and nuclear militarization likely will trigger additional regional nuclear proliferation. It is also likely to invite a preemptive attack from Israel, which Iranian leaders have repeatedly promised to obliterate.

Sunni actors will view any counter-terrorism measures taken by Israel as a threat to their own interests, and some among them may use such actions as a pretext for attacking this despised enemy, particularly as a durable caliphate seems closer to realization.

All told, the volatile region is facing a cascade of state failures. When – not if – that occurs, it will lead to the dissolution of state borders that will facilitate the establishment of a durable caliphate, which will span both continents[234]. This expansive terrorist entity will become a platform for launching a multi-faceted global jihad that will spawn insurrections within countries hosting Muslims. The goal will be to bring the West under Islam's control.

The region's Islamic movements are plugged into Asian and African diaspora communities that are settled in Western countries and hard-pressed by spillover effects stemming from conflicts back home. An unknown amount of funds these expatriate communities generate make it to terrorist groups engaged in the conflicts. These communities largely maintain insularity within their host societies, yet adjust to their Western cultures in order to function unimpeded as nodes in the global da'wa-to-jihad infrastructure, which is the principal vehicle for exporting the Islamic revolution. The youth within these expatriate communities, as well as the disaffected within the host societies, are prime targets for recruitment by Muslim terrorist groups seeking to attack the West. Toward this objective, Muslim terrorist groups are becoming more innovative, more capable, more connected, and more attractive.

Wealthy states from among the Arab-Muslim bloc, especially the Gulf States, are wont to keep these expatriate communities afloat in order to keep the da'wa-to-jihad infrastructure well-oiled in anticipation of the global caliphate. Saudi Arabia, for its part, has taken a lead position in heading up the exportation of the Sunni revolution: The Saudi royal family has built 1,500 mosques, 210 Islamic cultural centers, 202 colleges, and about 2,000 schools in non-Islamic countries from 1975 through 2003[235]. The House of Saud stocks these institutions with puritanical Wahhabi teachings, staffs them with the kingdom's unmanageable *ulama* or religious scholars, and sends its unruly militants abroad to fight in theaters of jihad where the kingdom's official policy to alleviate Muslim suffering translates into supporting jihadists and refugees in the conflict zones[236]. Bankrolling by Saudi Arabia and other wealthy Gulf states enables the da'wa-to-jihad infrastructure: a thick transcontinental Islamic web of expatriate communities, youth organizations, cultural centers, mosques, schools, compromised charities, legitimate and front businesses, *hawalas* and other banking systems, wealthy private donors, criminalized states, terrorist groups, and non-Muslim stakeholders operating in synergetic fashion toward advancing the global caliphate project while undermining the existing global order.

Meanwhile, on the heels of the Obama administration sanitizing all government training curriculum on Islamic terrorism, effectively neutering counter-terrorism training[237], and reprograming U.S. warfighters to be culturally literate[238], Western universities – many of which receive ample Saudi funding – are now hosting panel discussions over reviving the caliphate, featuring cherry picked visiting professors soft-peddling the concept to attentive Muslim students and their inquiring peers[239]. This, while *successful* attacks in the name of Allah on Western soil as of late have become bolder, more frequent, and increasingly lethal: from Little Rock, Arkansas [240] to Fort Hood, Texas [241] to Toulouse and Montauban, France [242] to Boston, Massachusetts [243] to London, United

Kingdom[244] to King County, Washington and Newark, New Jersey[245] to Brussels, Belgium[246] to Melbourne, Australia[247] to Moore, Oklahoma[248] to Quebec and Ottawa, Canada[249] to Queens, New York[250] to Washington D.C.[251] to Sydney, Australia[252] to Brooklyn, New York[253] to Paris and Montrouge, France[254]. These were attacks carried out in revenge for perceived injustices against Muslims, for U.S. counter-terrorism operations in the Middle East, for passport revocation of high-risk Muslims attempting to go overseas to answer call-ups for jihad, and for general refusal to convert to Islam.

CONCLUSION

The Commander-in-Chief of the U.S. forces and leader of the free world is dangerously misrepresenting Islam and peddling a delusion by declaring that IS is not Islamic.

Consider this representative hadith from Sahih Bukhari, whose hadith collections per the Islamic world are regarded as highly reliable and authoritative, and therefore widely respected and worthy of exemplifying:

> *"Narrated by Abu Huraira: A man came to Allah's Apostle and said, 'Instruct me as to such a deed as equals jihad (in reward).' He replied, 'I do not find such a deed.' Then he added, 'Can you, while the Muslim fighter is in the battle-field, enter your mosque to perform prayers without cease and fast and never break your fast?' The man said, 'But who can do that?' Abu-Huraira added, 'The Mujahid (i.e. Muslim fighter) is rewarded even for the footsteps of his horse while it wanders bout (for grazing) tied in a long rope.' "*

> *Sahih Bukhari Vol 4., book 52, hadith no. 44*

From the 7th century to the 21st century, Muhammad's faithful disciples have grasped his message: The greatest deed performed in the service of Allah is violent jihad, which holds out great rewards in this world and in the Islamic paradise hereafter. Jihad is a gateway straight to the Islamic paradise; it is the aspiration of the most loyal of Allah's slaves; and devotion to him occurs by turning the combat site into a place of Islamic worship[255]. Accordingly, Muslims have raided and plundered their way through more than 250 *major* campaigns and conquests[256].

That IS is conducting jihad in Syria and in Iraq – areas marking key historic Muslim battles[257] and portending apocalyptic End Time events[258] – to revive a caliphate in the tradition of the first four "rightly guided" caliphs that succeeded Muhammad lends unmistakable relevance and Islamic validity to this insurgent group's grisly and prosperous enterprise.

Jihadist groups undertaking caliphate projects and similar endeavors today are straightforwardly carrying out the tenets and the dictates of their religion – sanctified by Allah per the Qur'an and *Ahadith*, and confirmed by Muhammad's own example on waging offensive jihad.

> *"Narrated [by] Abu Huraira: The prophet said, 'By him in whose hands my life is! Were it not for some men amongst the believers who dislike to be left behind me and whom I cannot provide with means of conveyance, I would certainly never remain behind any Sariya' (army-unit) setting out in Allah's Cause. By him in whose hands my life is! I would love to be martyred in Allah's Cause and then get resurrected and then get martyred, and then get resurrected again and then get martyred and then get resurrected again and then get martyred.'"*

Sahih Bukhari Vol 4., book 52, hadith no. 54

The Islamic world understands well that Muhammad's later revelations calling for offensive jihad during the height of his spiritual adventurism and bloody campaigns abrogate his earlier seemingly conciliatory utterances that he delivered when he was just an oddity building up a following. Thus, in classic Muhammadan tradition, jihadists are jumping on the Caliphate Caravan and riding the groundswell of violent jihad to spread Allah's *deen* – path and religion – on the global road to conquest of non-Muslim peoples and their bounteous lands in this world, and to Allah's favor and untold fleshly delights in the next world.

Simply put: For non-Muslim societies, peace with Islam is a zero sum game.

Islam thus presents a *clear and present danger* to non-Muslim societies.

"Enmity and hatred have become manifest between you and us forever – until you believe in Allah."

Qur'an, surah 60:6

RECOMMENDATIONS

The piecemeal counter-terrorism approach to the growing Islamic terrorist threat is not sustainable in the regions discussed herein. A comprehensive strategy is needed to safeguard Western societies and other societies with similar systems of governance, which share the norms and values of upholding the rule of law, safeguarding human rights, promoting individual freedom with responsibility, respecting state sovereignty, and preserving the Judeo-Christian heritage. These societies are referred to hereafter as the Western bloc.

Deeply opposing value systems between the Western bloc and the Arab-Muslim bloc prevent these actors from launching a robust, coordinated, multidimensional response to address 21st century asymmetrical warfare waged by media savvy, globally networked, well-heeled hybrid terrorist organizations flouting international law. Alliances between these actors have been merely tactical and largely unreliable, and have left the Western bloc open to exploitation.

The following recommendations could contribute to a comprehensive strategy:

Recommendation 1

Rather than trying to nail down the ever-elusive internationally acceptable definition of terrorism, there should be a timely examination of multi-state definitions of terrorism that could be tapped and improved upon until achieving the best definition suitable for the Western bloc. The resulting definition should contain a provisional addendum for partner countries outside of the bloc to help them effectuate sound counter-terrorism strategies. Concurrently, there should be a new anti-terrorism alliance established to protect and advance the interests of the Western bloc, which would give the resulting definition teeth.

The advantages of this two-part program: (1) Existing foundational work upon which to build a definition of terrorism suitable for the Western bloc already exists[259]; (2) It bolsters synergy and coordination of member states and partners, regardless of individual capabilities, to launch defensive and offensive military actions against terrorist perpetrators and their sponsors; (3) Heightens the level of interoperability for threat assessments, readiness, rapid deployment, and rights of passage; (4) Improves collaborative real-time intelligence and counter-intelligence collection and sharing, reconnaissance and surveillance, and target acquisition; (5) Facilitates enterprise-level operations to heighten and disrupt terrorist movement, organization, planning, and implementation of attacks; (6) Encourages participating states to more equitably share the political, military, and economic burden involved in mitigating the threat; (7) More effectively frustrates terrorism fundraising activities and more effectively curtails the economic resources of those sponsoring terrorism; (8) Reduces vulnerability of critical infrastructure covering cyber security, transportation routes and facilities, postal routes, financial markets, water and energy resources, and communications systems; (9) Forges a way forward to address proliferation of air and sea piracy, and the hijacking of democracy by terror supporting societies; (10) Heightens the ability to implement non-proliferation programs, and to monitor the manufacturing, purchasing, storage, and movement of CBRN weapons and components; and (11) Enhances performance in the international, legal, political, and diplomatic spheres of influence to (a) devise terror-specific legislation to identify, punish, and monitor those states, organizations, and individuals engaged in or sponsoring terrorism; (b) hold accountable and demand transparency from states adhering to nebulous practices designed to circumvent Western counter-terrorism efforts; (c) develop standardized protocol and task forces to address threats and incidents involving transportation infrastructure, and to address special circumstances; (d) strengthen the ability to defend from terrorist attacks without fear of international condemnation and retribution, mitigate the damage caused by international organizations that target member states and partners, and open the door to expose their practices; (e) facilitate the media in developing best practices regarding coverage of terrorist incidents; (f) clarify and de-politicize terror-related education and training; and (g) add value and substance to partnerships to further Western values and to enhance defense in the areas of institution building, modernization, reform, and planning.

The disadvantages of this two-part program: (1) Belligerent non-member state and non-state actors will harden their battle-lines against the new alliance, which can increase threats and invite aggression; and (2) Some members may have more objections than other members over agenda items and alliance actions, and there may arise concerns vis-à-vis partnerships.

Recommendation 2

Decades of Iran's strategic deception, hardening of its nuclear posture, and sanctions-weathering activities juxtaposed with an international coordination problem means the global community will likely face a nuclear breakout capability of an Iranian regime headed by apocalyptic visionaries. Sunni-Shi'a competition to rule the Muslim world and to foist an Islamic system on non-Muslim nations will likely carry over to the nuclear realm. Saudi Arabia threatened to get the bomb from Pakistan if Iran weaponizes, but, as mentioned, Pakistan and its nuclear weapons may fall to terrorist hands. Regional sentiment indicates a Middle East heading for a nuclear arms race. Iran will try to prevent this by probing more avenues to extend its influence in the Sunni world in hopes of attaining at least a tactical arrangement to enable Muslims to stand as a unifying anti-Western force.

Nonproliferation regimes, relevant international forums, and agreeable UN Member States should leverage and pool their strategic assets and interactions in an all out effort to deliver a multifaceted response that would bring to bear all relevant tools of statecraft against targeted elements within Iran. At this late hour, however, such an effort would not likely yield the desired outcome. More sanctions would provide more fuel for supreme leader 'Ali Khamenei to stoke nationalist and religious sentiments, as he prepares Iranians to usher in the dangerous era of their version of a messianic figure called "Mahdi" by increasing Iran's defense spending, completing its nuclear weapons program, and enhancing its missile and space technology. A significant element of Iranian society supports nuclear weaponization.

The Western bloc should coordinate under a new anti-terrorism alliance, as proposed in Recommendation 1, and it should prepare for the likely eventualities of a nuclearized Iran, a Middle East mired in a nuclear arms race, and a subsequent erosion of the nonproliferation regime. This bloc should also prepare for the possibility that Hizb'allah – whose reach extends to 40 countries, including in the Western hemisphere – would be a recipient of at least one small implosion-type nuclear device from Iran.

Recommendation 3

Members of the Western bloc should develop and exchange notes on comprehensive risk and crisis communication programs designed to build national cultures of preparedness and vigilant publics resilient to terrorism. These programs should be dynamic, and should address ongoing problems with information flow, decision-making, inter-organizational coordination, and multilateral cooperation. The programs should feature multi-level educational programs; multilateral, national, state, and local drills; targeted training; and self-help tool-kits designed to empower the various publics to help themselves; first-responders; and, as applicable, other bloc members; before, during, and after manmade disasters and crises.

Recommendation 4

Members of the Western bloc that do not implement conscripted service should do so in order to relieve overburdened warfighters from recurring tours of duty; especially in countries like the U.S that carry the lion's share of the counter-terrorism burden. Such a program would put Western countries on war footing, which would condition their societies to function in a constant state of preparedness.

Recommendation 5

Instead of ineffective and dangerous denials that it is not enmeshed in a religious war, the Western bloc, in the interest of preserving its Judeo-Christian heritage, should acknowledge the undeniable religious component of the War on Terror, and should forthrightly address it as a decisive contest waged by an unyielding enemy bent on replacing the bloc's core historical and cultural traditions with Islam.

> *"Narrated 'Aisha and Ibn 'Abbas: 'On his death-bed Allah's apostle put a sheet over his face and when he felt hot, he would remove it from his face. When in that state (of putting and removing the sheet) he said, "May Allah's curse be on the Jews and Christians for they build places of worship at the graves of their prophets." (By that) he intended to warn (the Muslim) from what they (Jews and Christians) had done.' "*
>
> *Sahih Bukhari, Vol. 4, Book 56, No. 660*

Counter-*da'wa* multi-media campaigns, particularly from Christian organizations, should be launched to responsibly challenge Muslims to self-improvement – an important aspect of their internal jihad[260] – by comparing Qur'anic-based texts with Hebrew and Greek narratives from the Bible[261]. Muhammad, in order to legitimize his authority and develop a following, endorsed the Bible, but craftily distorted his selection of narratives therein, which he then claimed to be revelations and prophecies handed down to him by Allah[262]. This would become the Qur'an, or more accurately: The Generous Qur'an. Muhammad used the resulting derailed Biblical narratives to sanctify violence and hatred, which he then directed at those who failed to follow his prescription for redemption, even going to the extent of ordering that men and their homes be set on fire if they failed to show up for prayer[263]. Such directives enabled Muhammad to build a profitable enterprise among his faithful followers. Before he died, Muhammad made certain to leave to his disciples a legacy of hatred, particularly directed at Jews and Christians, which ensured that terrorism in the name of Islam would continue unabated.

Counter-*da'wa* campaigns should leverage the Internet, billboards, traditional media outlets, and social media. Such outreach efforts would provide Muslims with unfiltered voices of alternative morality that they otherwise would not likely hear. There are Muslims who have testified after embracing Christianity that they have undergone life-changing experiences, which have liberated them from ancient hostilities and hatred directed at Jews and at Christians, and which have enabled them to live peaceably amid non-Muslim communities.

It is important to be mindful when launching any counter-*da'wa* campaign that Muslims are entrapped in a cult of incessant death and destruction because they are bound by core Qur'anic texts that teach that Allah promotes human sacrifice accomplished via jihad against infidels as the ultimate way his slaves can demonstrate their worthiness to enter paradise and thus avoid hell fire and damnation. Therefore, counter-*da'wa* outreach efforts should be driven by compassion, and conducted using discernment and tact.

Other Recommendations

Psychological operations should be stepped up to exploit divisions that have arisen in the jihadi community and within individual terrorist organizations over AQ and IS and their respective caliphate projects. The rivalry between AQ and IS should be fully exploited.

Western countries should expand monitoring activities and passport revocation of their citizens going to Asia *and* to Africa to fight or to train. They should review their lists of visa waiver countries and adjust them appropriately, and should increase information sharing and coordination so that a dragnet is created to detect citizens who have gone to either of these continents to fight or to train, and who are trying to make their way back home.

Porous borders should be secured, and immigration laws should be revised to address understated threats destabilizing Western and Western-oriented societies, such as engineered demographic invasions, and spillover from war-ravaged countries.

International law should be brought into the 21st century to effectively address international piracy, which threatens international commerce; runaway self-determination, which erodes state sovereignty; and the hijacking of democratic elections, which allows terrorist groups to exploit state organs of power.

Crux of the Matter

Westerns would do well to grasp that anything that stands in the way of the propagation of Islam – a core Muslim duty – is considered oppression. A host country that acts in the interest of self-preservation, politically, militarily, or culturally, will be deemed an oppressor, which gives cause for waging jihad. Jihadists understand from their texts and from their role models that a pious Muslim finds a reason to wage jihad because it is considered a good deed of the highest order sanctified by Allah.

The call-up is beckoning: caliphate revival for Muslim survival. The caravan awaits another journey. Lawlessness is infectious, and the West's malcontents are taking note. The days of kicking the proverbial can down the road and refusing to see the writing on the wall must end if the Judeo-Christian heritage is to survive.

Suggestion for Future Research

In the process of examining the regions discussed herein, this author observed the following that was beyond the scope of this report to examine: In some apparent measure, terrorist groups therein are morphing into terrorist networks and terrorist syndicates with elastic and overlapping ties to criminal networks and compromised stakeholder organizations, as well as to an expanding Salafist Jihadist movement. Global connectivity, state cover, insufficient governmental capacity, lack of political will, and poor international coordination appear to be at least some enabling factors that are providing fertile ground for these evolving mega-terrorist entities to grow.

ABOUT THE AUTHOR

Sandra Warmoth is a recent M.A. graduate with honors of the Lauder School of Government, Diplomacy & Strategy, with a Specialization in Counter-Terrorism and Homeland Security via the International Institute for Counter-Terrorism, Herzliya, Israel. She also earned dual baccalaureate degrees with honors in Journalism and in Political Science: International Relations from the University of Central Florida, U.S. Her fields of study include – Regions: Asia and the Middle East, Africa, and Latin America: dynamics, threat assessments, ungoverned and under-governed spaces, criminalized and failing states; Special areas of study: Arab-Israeli conflict; Islam: fundamentalism, Muslim terrorist groups and terrorism, Islamic global agenda; nuclear weapons, unconventional terrorism. Sandra's graduate-level products were published in the *International Institute for Counter-Terrorism Working Paper Series*, and in the *Small Wars Journal*. Her graduate-level work was cited during expert testimony before the House of Representatives Subcommittee on Oversight, Investigations, and Management of the Committee on Homeland Security during the 112th Congress.

1 President Obama's behindhand four-point plan has initially called for (1) a systematic, open-
    ended campaign of targeted airstrikes against IS as Iraqi forces engage the terrorist
    organization in a ground offensive, and an expansion of the operation to Syria as necessary;
    (2) sending 475 U.S. service members to Iraq tasked with providing a supportive role to
    Iraqi and Kurdish forces fighting IS on the ground; (3) bringing to bear substantial counter-
    terrorism capabilities; shoring up international coordination and support, including via the
    United Nations Security Council; and tapping localized military forces in the Middle East
    theatre; (4) and providing more humanitarian assistance to threatened and displaced
    populations to ensure they return or remain in their ancient homelands. "Transcript:
    President Obama's Speech on Combating ISIS and Terrorism," White House transcript as
    presented by CNN, September 10, 2014,
    http://www.cnn.com/2014/09/10/politics/transcript-obama-syria-isis-speech/index.html

2 Since the 16th century, the Ottoman sultans laid claim to the coveted title "caliph of the
    Muslims." Founder and president of the Turkish Republic, Mustafa Kemal Atatürk, abolished
    the caliphate on March 3, 1924 as part of his program of sweeping reforms to bring his
    country into the 20th century. Encyclopaedia Britannica, "Kemal Ataturk: The Turkish
    Republic," last updated April 9, 2014,
    http://www.britannica.com/EBchecked/topic/40411/Kemal-Ataturk/24782/The-Turkish-
    republic

3 Ryan Mauro, "Al Qaeda Announces New Branch and Bid for Own Caliphate," The Clarion
    Project, September 4, 2014, http://www.clarionproject.org/analysis/al-qaeda-announces-
    new-branch-and-bid-own-caliphate

4 Elad Benari, "ISIS Declares an Islamic Caliphate," Arutz Sheva, June 30, 2014,
    http://www.israelnationalnews.com/News/News.aspx/182311#.VBEkgSjzj6k

5 The full text of the caliphate announcement is accessible via Bill Roggio of The Long War
    Journal, at http://myreader.toile-libre.org/uploads/My_53b039f00cb03.pdf

6 Al Nafir: a Call to Mobilize or a Call to Arms. Thomas Joscelyn, "Al Qaeda Renews its Oath of
    Allegiance to Taliban Leader Mullah Omar," The Long War Journal, July 21, 2014,
    http://www.longwarjournal.org/archives/2014/07/al_qaeda_renews_its-print.php

7 The Taliban in Afghanistan is used in conjunction with the Islamic Emirate in Afghanistan, a
    name derived from the group's rule in this country from 1996 to 2001. Jihadi Websites
    Monitoring Group, "Summary of Information on Jihadist Websites," bimonthly report, first
    half of June 2014, published October 19, 2014,

http://www.ict.org.il/Article/1232/Periodical_Review_Summary_from_the_Jihadi_Forums_T
he_First_Half_of_June_2014

8 Qaedat al-Jihad in the Indian Subcontinent also goes by the name: Al Qa'ida in the Indian
Subcontinent (AQIS)

9 Omar earned respect in the Islamic world for his endeavors to transform Afghanistan into the
"purest Islamic State" in the world via his founding of the Islamic Emirate of Afghanistan in
1996, where he imposed sharia law and remained detached from world affairs. He acquired
the title "Commander of the Faithful" after taking over Afghanistan that year, and ran the
country until he was toppled in 2001. Omar pursued his Islamic scholarship in several
Islamic schools and madrassas. He is the final authority in the Taliban hierarchy. The name
"Islamic Emirate of Afghanistan" traditionally depicts a localized designation as compared to
the expansive designation of a caliphate. The name resurfaced in 2013 when Taliban
representatives and Qatari officials caused a political flap because of an opening ceremony
for a Taliban office in Doha, Qatar that featured a poster with the group's formal name. The
move, it was said, was intended to open dialogue between the Taliban and the world rather
than a way to expand the group's territorial reach. Although traditionally the Taliban has
adhered to a local focus, AQ historically has endeavored to co-opt local jihads and to
globalize them, but not always with success. Associated Foreign Press, "Qatar Says Taliban
Office Not for 'Islamic Emirate,' " June 19, 2013, Fox News,
http://www.foxnews.com/world/2013/06/19/qatar-says-taliban-office-not-for-islamic-
emirate; AND Thomas Joscelyn, "Al Qaeda Renews its Oath of Allegiance to Taliban Leader
Mullah Omar," July 21, 2014, The Long War Journal,
http://www.longwarjournal.org/archives/2014/07/al_qaeda_renews_its-print.php; AND
South Asia Terrorism Portal, "Mullah Mohammed Omar," accessed September 10, 2014,
http://satp.org/satporgtp/usa/Mullah_Moh.htm

10 Dr. Abdullah Azzam mentored Usama Bin Laden, and was a key strategist behind global jihad.
Religious scholar and Muslim Brotherhood member, Azzam lectured at King 'Abd al-'Aziz
University in Jeddah, Saudi Arabia, where he promoted Salafia ideology, and elevated the
Muslim duty to wage jihad from the state level to the global level of the ummah, a concept he
developed in the 1980s. His fatwa, approved by the highest religious authority in Saudi
Arabia, Sheikh 'Abd al-'Aziz bin Baz, espoused the personal duty of every Muslim to take part
in jihad where Muslims are engaged in wars with those deemed enemies of Islam. Muslim
religious scholars are hard pressed to deny Abdullah Azzam's fatwa, as well as other
fundamentalist fatwas, because such rulings are grounded in the Qur'an; and in the Sunna on
the life of Islam's prophet, Muhammad, whom Muslims must emulate. The Sunna is set forth
in Ahadith: the traditions reporting on the sayings of Muhammad, what he did, what he
wore, and how he lived. The Qur'an and the Sunna are two main sources of sharia law: the

other two being consensus between respected religious scholars on legal questions, and analogy or self-conclusion based on the Qur'an and the Sunna. Azzam's fatwa draws its potency and relevance from the concurring opinions of four principal religious scholars: Hanafi, Maliki, Shafi'i, and Hanbali, who founded the four law schools of Islam. Azzam's goal was to establish the caliphate. He moved to Pakistan to teach at the International Islamic University in Islamabad, and was assassinated in 1989.

11 Ummah is a reference to the global Muslim community

12 Senior AQ in Pakistan member, Mawlana Asim Umar, in a video released back in June 2014, called on Muslims in Kashmir to wage jihad against the regime in India. Also, the Indian Navy placed its warships on high alert after AQIS in September 2014 attempted to hijack the Pakistani missile frigate, PNS Aslat, in order to attack the Indian vessels; and intelligence sources report that AQ launched a terror module to recruit jihadists in the area. Jihadi Websites Monitoring Group, "Summary of Information on Jihadist Websites," bimonthly report, first half of June 2014, published October 19, 2014, http://www.ict.org.il/Article/1232/Periodical_Review_Summary_from_the_Jihadi_Forums_T he_First_Half_of_June_2014; AND News Briefs, October 6-12, 2014, South Asia Intelligence Review, Vol. 13, No. 15, http://www.satp.org/satporgtp/sair/Archives/sair13/13_15.htm

13 Thomas Joscelyn, "Al Qaeda in the Indian Subcontinent Calls for Jihadist Unity Against US-led Coalition," November 4, 2014, The Long War Journal, http://www.longwarjournal.org/archives/2014/11/al_qaeda_in_the_indi_2-print.php

14 Al-Baghadadi is former leader of IS forerunner, Islamic State of Iraq, a front for AQ in Iraq. The Islamic State of Iraq was notorious for its extreme brutality, such that it tarnished the AQ brand in the Muslim world. "Iraqi Insurgent Group Names New Leaders," by Anthony Shadid, May 16, 2010, The New York Times, http://atwar.blogs.nytimes.com/2010/05/16/iraqi-insurgent-group-names-new-leaders/?_php=true&_type=blogs&_r=1; AND "Who is ISIS Leader Abu Bakr al-Baghdadi?" by Janine Di Giovanni, Newsweek, December 8, 2014, http://www.newsweek.com/2014/12/19/who-isis-leader-abu-bakr-al-baghdadi-290081.html

15 Abu Bakr al-Baghadadi is thought to be a descendant from the Islamic prophet Muhammad's Quraysh tribe, which is considered a core qualification for the office of the caliphate; and his PhD from the University of Baghdad with a concentration on Islamic jurisprudence, sharia, history, and culture has conferred upon him a degree of legitimacy that according to his supporters makes him worthy of the position of caliph. "ISIS Jihadists Declare 'Islamic Caliphate,' " Al Arabia News, June 29, 2014, http://english.alarabiya.net/en/News/2014/06/29/ISIS-jihadists-declare-caliphate-.html;

AND Aaron Y. Zelin, "Abu Bakr al-Baghdadi: Islamic State's Driving Force," July 30, 2014, Washington Institute for Near East Policy, as presented by BBC News, http://www.bbc.com/news/world-middle-east-28560449?print=true

16 African Armed Forces journal, "ISIS Divides Maghreb Al-Qaeda (AQIM)," August 19, 2014, http://www.aafonline.co.za/news/isis-divides-maghreb-al-qaeda-aqim

17 Since July 2014, there have been several occasions where al-Baghdadi was reported killed in airstrikes, including reports from Turkish and Kurdish officials, and they were proven wrong. "Isis Video 'Shows al-Baghdadi Alive' After Death Rumors," July 5, 2014, BBC News, http://www.bbc.com/news/world-middle-east-28178272; AND "URGENT: Death of ISIS Leader Abu Bakr al-Baghdadi Denied by Iraqi, US Sources," September 8, 2014, Iraqi News, http://www.iraqinews.com/iraq-war/urgent-isis-leader-abu-bakr-al-baghdadi-remains-alive; AND "Islamic State Leader al-Baghdadi Still Alive but Other Leaders Killed," December 18, 2014, Reuters, Newsweek, http://www.newsweek.com/report-islamic-state-leaders-killed-airstrikes-293263

18 Rita Katz, "IS Releases Five Statements of Allegiance to Abu Bakr al-Baghdadi Within 24 Hours," SITE Intelligence Group, https://news.siteintelgroup.com/blog/index.php/entry/308-is-releases-five-statements-of-allegiance-to-abu-bakr-al-baghdadi-in-24-hours

19 CBS News, "Purported New ISIS Audio Tape Surfaces," http://www.cbsnews.com/videos/purported-new-isis-audio-tape-surfaces; AND Thomas Joscelyn, "Islamic State Leader Claims 'Caliphate' Has Expanded in New Audio Message," November 13, 2014, The Long War Journal, http://defenddemocracy.org/media-hit/thomas-joscelyn-islamic-state-leader-claims-caliphate-has-expanded-in-new-audio-message; AND Aaron Y. Zelin, "The Islamic State's Archipelago of Provinces," November 14, 2014, The Washington Institute for Near East Policy, http://www.washingtoninstitute.org/policy-analysis/view/the-islamic-states-archipelago-of-provinces

20 See page 6 of the caliphate announcement, accessible at The Long War Journal, http://myreader.toile-libre.org/uploads/My_53b039f00cb03.pdf

21 "Islamic State Leader al-Baghdadi Still Alive but Other Leaders Killed," by Reuters, December 18, 2014, Newsweek, http://www.newsweek.com/report-islamic-state-leaders-killed-airstrikes-293263?piano_t=1

22 Saudi Arabia holds 25% of the world's oil reserves, making the kingdom a prime target for IS operations. Although there are safeguards in place to bolster the Saudi Arabia's energy security, successful IS penetration into the kingdom's energy infrastructure would not only further enrich and empower this terrorist entity and destabilize a significant portion of the

world's oil supply, it would cause fierce Sunni-Shi'a fighting to erupt, especially in the
Eastern Province, which would draw Iran into the conflict. Saudi Arabia's Eastern Province is
dominated by a long-oppressed, restive Shi'a populace that has been calling for secession of
this area, the most oil rich region in the world. The province is in close proximity to the
largest sea port in the Persian Gulf, Dammam's King Abdul Sea Port; the largest industrial
city in the Middle East, Jubail; and major refinery operations involving the kingdom-owned
oil company Saudi Aramco, the largest in the world. The kingdom has experienced attacks
against its facilities. In 2004, a deadly terrorist attack on the kingdom's Yanbu petrochemical
plant was isolated when Saudi security cordoned off its industrial section and killed the
intruders. In February 2006, AQ terrorists attacked the kingdom's large Abqaiq oil complex,
the world's largest crude stabilization facility and nerve center of the Saudi distribution
system, killing the guards, breaching the outer perimeter, and detonating a car bomb in the
buffer area within which they were trapped. "Oil, the Present and Future," Saudi Arabia
Market Information Resource, http://www.saudinf.com/main/x006.htm; AND Joshua
Teitelbaum, "Sunni vs. Shiite in Saudi Arabia," January 16, 2011, Jerusalem Center for Public
Affairs, Hoover Institution, http://www.hoover.org/research/sunni-vs-shiite-saudi-arabia;
AND Nawaf Obaid, "The Day of Saudi Collapse is Not Near," April 13, 2011

23 An attack against al-Suweif border fortification, 25 miles from the town of Arar, Saudi Arabia,
where four Saudi-born IS operatives advancing from within Iraq opened fire on the northern
border patrol on January 5, 2015, created a skirmish, and an explosion when one of the
attackers detonated his suicide belt upon capture. The attack killed General Oudah al-Belawi,
commander of border operations in Saudi Arabia's northern zone, and two other guards.
This was the first direct attack on Saudi armed forces by IS, which claimed the oil rich
kingdom for its caliphate. The attack took place nearby an area largely under IS control.
Saudi police also blamed IS for an attack on the kingdom's Shi'a community in al-Ahsa
province that killed eight in November 2014. There have been long-range mortar attacks
that have come over the border into the kingdom. Such attacks threaten the kingdom's
stability, illuminate a fifth column of IS adherents therein, stoke hostilities between Sunnis
and Shiites, and leave Saudi Arabia's numerous oil and gas fields and refineries vulnerable.
The drive along main routes from Arar to Saudi Arabia's Ghawar Oil Field is around 10 hours
and 39 minutes, and much of the area is open desert and sparsely populated, making for easy
advancement of hostile actors. The Ghawar Oil Field belongs to state-owned Saudi Aramco,
and is the world's largest oil field both by oil reserves and production. It is situated in the
eastern part of the Empty Quarter desert, underlying 1.3 million acres, along the western
Gulf coast. The onshore oil field comprises five development areas: Ain Dar, Haradh,
Uthmaniya, Shedgum, and Hawiyah. This oil field is located in the Eastern Province, where
Shi'a unrest persists in the vast oil rich region. Sources: "ISIS Claims Attack on Saudi Arabia
Border, Signals Strategy Change in Militant Infiltration," by Alessandria Masi, January 5,

2015, International Business Times, http://www.ibtimes.com/isis-claims-attack-saudi-arabia-border-signals-strategy-change-militant-infiltration-1773754; AND "Saudi General 'Killed in Attack on Border with Isil-held Iraq' " by Richard Spencer, January 5, 2015, The Telegraph, http://www.telegraph.co.uk/news/worldnews/middleeast/saudiarabia/11325032/Saudi-general-killed-in-attack-on-border-with-Isil-held-Iraq.html; AND "Ghawar Oil Field, Saudi Arabia, Hydrocarbons Technology Market & Consumer Insight, accessed January 23, 2015, http://www.hydrocarbons-technology.com/projects/ghawar-oil-field; AND Google Maps, accessed January 23, 2015, https://maps.google.com; AND "Oil, the Present and the Future," Saudi Arabia Market Information Resource, accessed January 23, 2015, http://www.saudinf.com/main/x006.htm; AND "Oil Markets Seek Stability Under New Saudi King Salman. A Short Price Spurt Followed Abdullah's Death," DEBKAfile, January 23, 2015, http://www.debka.com/article/24358

24 Sidebar: The newly crowned King Salman, who replaces the late King Abdullah, maintains a good reputation for being a family conciliator, hardworking, and not given to corruption. Lest it be forgotten, official records have demonstrated that he and his new deputy crown prince, half-brother Nayef, have been financial and ideological supporters of terrorism. Official Saudi support of jihadist activities have been accomplished via committees and charities, which have obscured the royal family's direct link to financing terrorism even beyond the oversight and directives of Salman and Nayef. This brief highlights Salman and Nayef, and asks the timely and timeless question: Does a leopard change its spots? The brief draws from a July 2003 report by The Middle East Media Research Institute, which informed on official Saudi documents, and from a July 2003 congressional hearing on terrorism financing before the Committee on Governmental Affairs of the U.S. Senate: From at least the period from 1998 to 2003, then prince Salmon, at the time governor of Riyadh Province, headed The Popular Committee for Assisting the Palestinian Mujahideen; and then prince Nayef, at the time Minister of Interior, headed The Support Committee for the Al-Quds Intifada, as well as The Al-Aqsa Fund. This money amply supplied a jihadi "martyrs fund," provided stipends to the families of jihadi "martyrs," and enabled terrorism directed against Israel. Royal orders were issued on their watch to launch fundraising campaigns to support the intifada terrorist campaign against Israel. The relentless campaign of terrorism against Israel is designed to dislodge the Jewish presence from the Arab and Muslim controlled strategic Fertile Crescent region with the goal of tying together Asia and Africa to create a caliphate. The Saudi monies made their way to the terrorist organization HAMAS via funding directed to front organizations like al-Jamiya al-Islamiya, which in 2001 trained 1,650 uniformed kindergarten students in the Gaza Strip, many with suicide belts, to re-enact terrorist attacks. Many of those children are now well-indoctrinated adults and quite literally ticking time bombs. Because of official U.S. sentiment of not wanting to upset and

embarrass the royal family, the House of Saud has managed to escape the wrath of U.S. sanctions targeting Saudi Arabia as a state supporter of terrorism, even though extending back to the 1990s the kingdom has also supported other terrorist groups, such as the Taliban; and even though Saudi government officials have routinely contributed large sums of money to corrupt and compromised Muslim charities that have supported terrorism. Before the May 12, 2003 bombing attacks by AQ against Riyadh, the royal family was quite uncooperative with U.S. counter-terrorism efforts: this because support for terrorism permeates the religious, ideological, educational, and financial sectors of the kingdom. Under heightened international scrutiny and following the 2003 bombings, the Saudi royal family began implementing a posh program to rehabilitate jihadists, the effectiveness of which has since been publicly questioned. The House of Saud's counter-terrorism efforts since the 2003 attacks have been mono-focused on how terrorism directly impacts its own kingdom. A national intelligence assessment from Israel that was brought up during the congressional hearing indicated that after the 2003 attacks, Saudi support for HAMAS actually was on the increase rather than on the decline. The Saudi official party line has been to deny supporting terrorism, yet, to support all efforts – including jihad – to liberate purported occupied land within Israel. Israel is internationally and legally recognized as the ancient ancestral homeland of the Jews, who have one country, whereas Muslims and Arabs already have 57. The official Saudi sentiment of supporting terrorism is rooted in Saudi Arabia's founding, and in the kingdom's foundational puritanical Salafia Wahhabist tradition, which is built upon the Qur'an and the Sunnah. Wahhabism is the fruit of an alliance in 1745 between Central Arabian sheikh Muhammad ibn Saud and Muslim preacher Muhammad bin Abdul Wahab, which resulted in a campaign of religious purification and conquest that led to the first Saudi state. Indeed, the inscription on Saudi Arabia's flag speaks of faith in Allah and the Islamic prophet Muhammad, its green backdrop elevates Wahhabism, and its sword pays tribute to the country's military prowess, its modern-day founding father, the late King Abdulaziz Ibn Saud, and the ruling al-Saud family in Allah's service. Saudi Arabia is the leading exporter of puritanical Salafia Wahhabism that drives global jihad. "Saudi Royal Family's Financial Support to the Palestinians 1998-2003: More than 15 Billion Riyals ($4 Billion U.S.) Given to 'Mujahideen Fighters' and 'Families of Martyrs,' " by Steven Stalinsky, July 3, 2003, The Middle East Media Research Institute, http://www.memri.org/report/en/print902.htm; AND "Terrorism Financing: Origination, Organization, and Prevention," Hearing before the Committee on Governmental Affairs, United States Senate, 108th Congress, First Session, July 31, 20013, 89-039 PDF, U.S. Government Printing Office, 2004.

25 Saudi King Abdullah's death comes on the heels of a series of deaths in the royal family and on the subsequent naming of crown princes, which occurred in rapid succession. The succession line is breaking down because succession in the kingdom is grounded in age-

based seniority, and passes from brother to brother among the sons of the late King Abdulaziz Ibn Saud, founding monarch of Saudi Arabia, who died in 1953. Many of Abdullah's surviving sons in the royal family range in age from the 70s through 80s, and are in poor health. Upon Abdullah's death on January 23, 2015, his brother Salman became king, however he is 79, in poor health, and has suffered a stroke. King Salmon's half-brother Muqrin, who is 69, is now crown prince, and widely believed to be the last capable son of Ibn Saud. In addition to 44 official sons, Ibn Saud had unofficial sons and numerous daughters – his offspring the product of 22 wives, plus concubines, and companions. The new King Salman named another of his half-brothers, Nayef, age 55, as deputy crown prince, which places this particular sibling second in line to the throne after Muqrin; and transfers future succession to the third generation of the House of Saud, thereby maintaining the custom of alternating the throne between offspring of the royal family who come from the Sudeiri and non-Sudeiri branches. King Salman and half-brother Mohammed are Sudeiris, while Muqrin and the recently passed Abdullah are non-Sudeiris. The move keeps peace among rival factions in the royal house, and may help to narrow the widening generation gap between the geriatric royal family and its subjects; however, it remains to be seen how the third generation of the House of Saud will perform upon taking the reigns. Abdullah had no full brothers and consequently had to forge alliances with others within the broader royal family, which includes at least 6,000 princes. In all, there are around 7,000 members of the royal al-Saud family, and about 700 are direct descendants of Ibn Saud. "After King Abdullah: Succession in Saudi Arabia," by Simon Henderson, Policy Focus #96, The Washington Institute for Near East Policy, August 2009, http://www.washingtoninstitute.org/policy-analysis/view/after-king-abdullah-succession-in-saudi-arabia; AND Royal Embassy of Saudi Arabia, Washington, D.C., Council of Ministers: Membership, accessed January 10, 2013, http://www.saudiembassy.net/print/about/Biographies-of-ministers.aspx; AND "Succession in Saudi Arabia: Salman's Ascension Promises Continuity at a Time of Regional Crisis," by Bruce Riedel, January 22, 2015, http://www.brookings.edu/blogs/markaz/posts/2015/01/22-saudi-abdullah-death-crown-prince-salman-successor; AND "Saudi King Abdullah Dies, New Ruler is Salman," by Angus McDowall and Ahmed Tolba, January 23, 2015, Reuters, http://www.reuters.com/article/2015/01/23/us-saudi-succession-idUSKBN0KV2RQ20150123; AND "Oil Markets Seek Stability Under New Saudi King Salman. A Short Price Spurt Followed Abdullah's Death," DEBKAfile, January 23, 2015, http://www.debka.com/article/24358

26 Saudi Arabia shares a lengthy border with Yemen, a battle-torn, impoverished country. Elevated instability in Yemen poses a strategic threat to Saudi Arabia; particularly because it gives space for Iran to further strengthen its toehold inside Yemen, which has a clear minority Shi'ite population of about 30 percent, even as it strengthens its foothold in Iraq,

which has a Shi'ite majority population of about 65 percent. Iran is situated just across the Persian Gulf from the Saudi kingdom, which has a sizeable Shi'ite minority of around 11 percent; and Iran has a foothold in Bahrain, which has a Shi'ite majority of around 70 percent. Sponsoring and riding a rise in Shi'a activism, Iran is expanding it influence and presence in these countries and in several other countries in the region. Consequently, there is a growing Shi'ite crescent in the region taking on the formation of a pincer maneuver cradling Saudi Arabia. Instability in Yemen also gives space for the Yemen-based Al Qaeda in the Arabian Peninsula to further expand its insurgency in this country, which could spill over into the Saudi kingdom. Yemen's youth-driven uprising in 2011, co-opted by elites and characterized by growing sectarianism, opened the door for a full-blown AQAP insurgency in Yemen. Also, a humanitarian crisis in Yemen unfolded due to escalating violence there that began in 2004 between a prominent Zaydi family, the Houthis, and Yemen's central government, which caused migrants to flee across the border into the Saudi kingdom. The Saudi royal family in 2013 constructed a barrier 1,100 miles long along its southern border with Yemen, and it is currently constructing a 600-mile long wall, compete with watchtowers, along its northern border with Iraq. Al-Saud has also been sending significant aid packages to help stabilize Yemen's economy and assist development efforts, and it collaborates with the U.S. in the latter's unpopular counter-terrorism campaign in Yemen. There have been past disputes between Yemen and Saudi Arabia over territory and potentially lucrative oil deposits, and north and south Yemenis expressed fear that the House of Saud had designs to annex the historical Hadramawt region to give the kingdom direct access to the Gulf of Aden. "Zaydi Revival in a Hostile Republic: Competing Identities, Loyalties, and Visions of State in Republican Yemen," by James Robin King, 2012, Arabica, Volume 59, Issue 3-4, pages 404-445, http://dx.doi.org/10.1163/157005812X629301; AND Personal communications, Shaul Mishal, PhD., Director, Middle East Division, Lauder School of Government, Diplomacy and Strategy, IDC Herzliya, December 26, 2012; AND "Saudi Arabian Jets 'Aiding US Strikes on Yemen,' " January 4, 2013, The Telegraph, http://www.telegraph.co.uk/news/worldnews/middleeast/saudiarabia/9779590/Saudi-Arabian-jets-aiding-US-strikes-on-Yemen.html; AND "Saudi Arabia Constructing 600-mile Wall to keep out ISIS," by Damian Sharkov, January 15, 2015, http://www.newsweek.com/saudi-arabia-constructing-600-mile-long-wall-keep-isis-out-299664

27 President Abed Rabbo Mansour Hadi and his cabinet resigned after a January 22, 2015 apparent coup attempt by the Houthi rebels, and government officials said he lost control over the military and intelligence agencies, which coordinate with the U.S. in counter-terrorism operations against AQAP. Yemen's Prime Minister Khaled Bahah also stepped down after the Houthis besieged his palace that same week. The resignation came after a power-sharing agreement to extend Houthi control over Yemen quickly unraveled. This

development is likely to have a bearing on the U.S. drone campaign in this country, unpopular due to resulting civilian casualties. The Houthi tribes, moreover, apparently are preparing at this writing to advance on central Marib, Yemen's main oil and gas region, as they reportedly tried to seize an army base 90 miles away. The security gap created by these developments is likely to result in greater Iranian involvement in Yemen, an intensification of AQAP's insurgency in the country, and it has the potential to lead to civil war. "Yemeni President, Cabinet Resign, Deepening Turmoil for a Key U.S. Ally," by Ali al-Mujahed and Hugh Naylor, January 22, 2015, The Washington Post, http://www.washingtonpost.com/world/aden-ports-reopened-but-rebels-still-outside-presidential-palace-and-residence/2015/01/22/d3563d88-a1ba-11e4-91fc-7dff95a14458_story.html

28 For instance, Sahih Bukhari, Vol. 4, Book 52, No. 177 beckons: "Narrated Abu Huraira: 'Allah's apostle said, "The Hour will not be established until you fight with the Jews, and the stone behind which a Jew will be hiding will say, 'O Muslim! There is a Jew hiding behind me, so kill him.' " ' "

29 Algeria is the economic engine of North Africa, and Europe's third largest gas supplier and major supplier of high quality crude oil. In January 2013, breakaway AQIM faction, al-Mouwakoune Bi-Dima, Those Who Sign in Blood, re-energized the global jihad when this small Sahel combat unit overran the remote, heavily guarded In Amenas gas field close to the Libyan border, killing at least 38 foreign workers at the plant.

30 After nearly three years of pinprick attacks and kidnappings, AQIM launched a deadly attack in April 2014 that brought it back to its lethality level of 2011 in Algeria. Terrorism Research & Analysis Consortium, "Al Qaeda in the Lands of the Islamic Maghreb," accessed November 16, 2014, http://www.trackingterrorism.org/group/al-qaeda-lands-islamic-maghreb-aqim-salafist-group-preaching-and-fighting-see-separate-entry

31 AQIM has been targeting officials, troops, police, international and government buildings, multinational corporations, and civilians since 2007.

32 AQIM wants its caliphate to include wide-ranging areas of the Maghreb, and of the Sahel where it has a foothold, and Spain and France. United Nations Security Council (UNSC) Al-Qaida and Taliban Sanctions Committee (1267) List, "The Organization of Al-Qaida in the Islamic Maghreb," updated September 9, 2014, http://www.un.org/sc/committees/1267/NSQE01401E.shtm; AND Zachary Laub and Jonathan Masters, "Backgrounder: Al-Qaeda in the Islamic Maghreb," Updated Jan. 8, 2014, Council on Foreign Relations, http://www.cfr.org/terrorist-organizations-and-networks/al-qaeda-islamic-maghreb-aqim/p12717

33 Thomas Joscelyn, "Islamic State Leader Claims 'Caliphate' Has Expanded in New Audio Message," November 13, 2014, http://defenddemocracy.org/media-hit/thomas-joscelyn-islamic-state-leader-claims-caliphate-has-expanded-in-new-audio-message

34 IS has been distributing booklets entitled "Fatah" or victory in Pashto and Dari, and it has support from a number of hardline groups operating in the border areas with Afghanistan, according to Press Trust of India, in "After Syria and Iraq, AfPak on Islamic State Radar," September 3, 2014, http://www.thehindu.com/news/international/south-asia/after-syria-and-iraq-afpak-on-islamic-state-radar/article6376654.ece?css=print; AND Bill Roggio and Thomas Joscelyn, "Discord Dissolves Pakistani Taliban Coalition," October 18, 2014, The Long War Journal, retrieved from http://defenddemocracy.org/media-hit/bill-roggio-discord-dissolves-pakistani-taliban-coalition

35 Synopsis of Abdul Rahim Muslim Dost: Dost is a citizen of Afghanistan who has used several aliases. He was a member of Jamaat ud Dawa il al Quran al Sunnat (JDQ), a little-known Salafist terror group that formally merged with the Taliban in January 2010, and which swore allegiance to Mullah Omar, and waged jihad in Afghanistan's Kunar province, a haven for AQ and allied terror groups. JDQ conducted training with several types of weapons in the Abdullah Abu Masood camp in Afghanistan. In addition to being a militant religious school that trains students in military camps and classrooms, JDQ has a militant wing and an assassination wing. Dost was reportedly an AQ point of contact in Herat, western Afghanistan. He also worked as a journalist for pro-Taliban publications, and is described as a "poet." Poetry is a prized traditional activity in jihadi camps, and the most expressive poets are considered to have special spiritual traits. Dost has several chronic conditions; therefore he is most suited for terrorist propaganda activities. Sources: A previously unclassified Combatant Status Review Board report dated September 29, 2004, and previously secret information released on June 27, 2004 by the U.S. Department of Defense Joint Task Force Guantanamo, both of which are archived on-line in "The Guantanamo Docket" compiled by The New York Times at http://projects.nytimes.com/guantanamo/detainees/561-abdul-rahim-muslim-dost; AND "US Targets Salafist Group Allied With the Taliban in Kunar, by Bill Roggio, August 19, 2010, The Long War Journal, http://www.longwarjournal.org/archives/2010/08/us_targets_salafist-print.php:

36 Dost's oath was released on July 1, 2014. He is believed to be behind a graffiti campaign to spread pro-IS messages throughout northern Pakistan. A Pakistani newspaper, Dawn, reported that Dost was named head of IS's presence in "Khorasan," which covers much of Central and South Asia, including Pakistan, Afghanistan, and Iran. Thomas Joscelyn, "Ex-Gitmo 'Poet' Now Recruiting for the Islamic State in Afghanistan and Pakistan," The Long War Journal, http://www.longwarjournal.org/archives/2014/11/ex-gitmo_poet_now_re-print.php

37 Two men share commonalities in their names as recorded in The New York Times'
  Guantanamo Docket. Synopses of both men appear here. The first man is associated in the
  files with the name "Mullah Abdul Rauf," but denied the association and said there are many
  in Afghanistan who go by this name. After reviewing the dockets, and news articles (one
  referenced here, and one by The Long War Journal appearing later regarding "Mullah Abdul
  Rauf Khadim" installed as governor of an IS province), it is likely that the man presented in
  Synopsis #1 is the "Mullah Abdul Rauf" noted by the Afghan officials. Synopsis #1 – Abdul
  Rauf Aliza: The Guantanamo Bay docket file on Rauf Aliza shows Mullah Abdul Rauf as an
  alternate name, not an alias. He apparently has no passport, and he claimed he lived in
  Afghanistan all his life. Rauf claimed that he entered into conscripted service for the Taliban
  against his will, and that he worked for its military delivering bread to troops because of a
  handicap that precluded his service as a regular soldier. However, his reference name,
  Mullah Abdul Rauf, was located on a list of factions and leaders within the Taliban as a corps
  commander in Herat, Afghanistan. Several other Guantanamo Bay detainees also identified
  him as a Taliban troop commander, which he denies. According to The New York Times,
  Amir Mohammad Akundzada, reportedly Rauf's relative and governor of Nimroz province
  neighboring Helmand, informed that Rauf served as a corps commander during the Taliban's
  1996-2001 rule of Afghanistan. Akundzada and General Mahmood Khan, deputy commander
  of the Afghan National Army's 215 Corps, said Rauf might have had a falling out with the
  leaders of the Afghan Taliban after spending time in the Pakistani city of Quetta, where it is
  believed that senior Taliban leaders are based. During interrogation at Guantanamo Bay,
  Rauf was said to be evasive regarding his role and leadership within the Taliban.
  Observations by analysts noted in various reviews that Rauf accurately identified top-level
  Taliban members, became closely associated with several senior level Taliban commanders
  and leaders, and exhibited leadership qualities by conducting speeches and instilling fear
  into those who cooperated with Joint Task Force Guantanamo Bay personnel. Another
  Guantanamo Bay detainee identified Rauf as a one time Taliban Governor of Herat,
  Afghanistan. Rauf admitted to his involvement in the production and sales of opium, and to
  his associations with criminal elements within the Taliban and Northern Alliance, but he
  refused to elaborate. There are intelligence gaps in his story, such as his involvement and
  knowledge concerning Taliban communications operations, his associations with other
  fellow detainees, and his opium business. It was noted that after serving three tours with
  Taliban, it did not seem plausible that he was not promoted and given more important duty.
  Also noted was that Rauf employed common anti-interrogation techniques used by other
  detainees, and by AQ. His intelligence value was upgraded from low to medium because of
  his possible knowledge of Taliban leadership and Command and Control. According to other
  information in his docket, Rauf joined the Taliban in 1998 in Kandahar, Afghanistan, and
  received training on the Kalishnikov rifle, which he denies. He stayed for more than a year at

a Taliban guesthouse, which he said was involuntarily and for only six weeks, where he worked for the Taliban military. His duties were believed to have included guarding a communication building in Konduz, and monitoring a radio and receiving updates on fighting in the area by local Taliban soldiers. Rauf claimed his role at this facility was serving food to the Taliban who were in the building, and although he overheard radio communications there, he never monitored radio transmissions. According to the documents, Rauf fought against the U.S. or its coalition partners, and he was in possession of a Kalishnikov rifle when he surrendered to Dostrum's Northern Alliance troops. Sources for Synopsis #1: An examination of the various documents in the Guantanamo Bay docket of Abdul Rauf Aliza can be accessed at: "The Guantanamo Docket" compiled by The New York Times, at http://projects.nytimes.com/guantanamo/detainees/108-abdul-rauf-aliza. The Guantanamo documents used for this synopsis include: "JTF-GTMO Assessment," October 26, 2004, U.S. Department of Defense Joint Task Force Guantanamo; AND "Administrative Review Board Round 1 Summaries," Department of Defense, Office for the Administrative Review of the Detention of Enemy Combatants at US Naval Base Guantanamo Bay, DMO-1, # 000990, no date; AND "Administrative Review Board Round 1 Transcripts," unclassified, ISN 108, Enclosure (5), # 000874; AND "Combatant Status Review Tribunal Transcripts," Unclassified/FOUO, ISN #108, Enclosure (3), #003478; AND "Combatant Status Review Tribunals Summaries," Combatant Status Review Board, August 17, 2004, Exhibit R-1, # 000121. The news article used for this synopsis: "Afghan Officials: Islamic State Group Operating in the South," by The Associated Press, January 12, 2015, The New York Times, http://www.nytimes.com/aponline/2015/01/12/world/asia/ap-as-afghanistan-islamic-state.html. Synopsis #2 – Abdul Rauf Omar Mohammed Abu al Qusin: Rauf is a citizen of Libya who has used several aliases and false passports. He is a seasoned jihadist with several years of formal military training on small weapons and communications, and he served in the Libyan Republican Guard/Army, but deserted in 1990. He began fighting with the Taliban in Afghanistan at the end of 1990, and received education and training in anti-aircraft systems at the Filipino Samar Khalia terrorist camp in Afghanistan; and also training in mortars, armor, and sniper rifles while fighting with the Libyan Islamic Fighting Group and other terrorist organizations. He enjoyed sponsorship from AQ, the Taliban, and the Libyan Islamic Fighting Group. His ties with other Guantanamo detainees, who have extensive educational and military backgrounds, predate their detention, and he is deeply networked in Afghanistan. He has knowledge of travel routes through Libya, Pakistan, and Afghanistan, and he knows the locations of jihadi guesthouses in the region. He was previously treated for psychosis. Source: Previously secret information released on September 24, 2004 by the U.S. Department of Defense Joint Task Force Guantanamo, which is archived on-line in "The Guantanamo Docket" compiled by The New York Times at http://projects.nytimes.com/guantanamo/detainees/709-abdul-rauf-omar-mohammed-abu-al-qusin

38 Reports from January 2014 indicate that up to 20 people were killed in fighting between the Taliban and IS, according to Saifullah Sanginwal, a tribal leader in the Sangin district. "Afghan Official: IS Operating in Helmand Province," by Rahim Faiez for The Associate Press, January 12, 2015, Marine Corps Times, http://www.marinecorpstimes.com/story/military/2015/01/12/islamic-state-group-operating-in-southern-helmand-province/21632705

39 Camps Leatherneck and Bastion, located in Helmand province, were shared by U.S. and British forces before they were formally handed over to Afghan forces on October 26, 2014, as part of the planned withdrawal of most foreign combat troops from Afghanistan by December 31, 2014. The sprawling 6,500-acre compound served as a crucial base to facilitate the fight against the Taliban in Afghanistan. The base once housed around 40,000 U.S. and allied troops, and the camps comprised a logistical hub and headquarters. Some of the fiercest fighting took place in Helmand, and most of the 378 U.S. Marines killed in this war lost their lives in this province. The British lost around 450 people, most of them in Helmand province. Leatherneck was the last operational base that the Marines oversaw in Afghanistan during this war, however some of the U.S. Marines stationed there remained to serve in an advisory capacity. Although the October 26, 2014 departure of the U.S. Marines and the last British combat troops marked the end of their role in this 13-year war, triggered by the September 11, 2001 attacks on the U.S. homeland, NATO Secretary-General Jens Stoltenberg declared the war over on December 28, 2014. Since then, the war has transitioned into a non-combat role for NATO, and there are around 12,000 NATO and partner-nation personnel that remain to train, advise, and assist Afghanistan's 350,000 soldiers. "Last of U.S. Marines Leave Afghanistan's Helmand Province," by Margherita Stancati, updated October 27, 2014, The Wall Street Journal, http://www.wsj.com/articles/last-of-u-s-marines-leave-afghanistans-helmand-province-1414410005; AND "War in Afghanistan Ends Combat Formally, Enters New Phase," by Andrew V. Pestano, December 28, 2014, http://www.upi.com/Top_News/World-News/2014/12/28/War-in-Afghanistan-ends-combat-formally-enters-new-phase/1431419789612

40 "Spies Warned White House: Don't Hit Al Qaeda in Syria," by Shane Harris and Jamie Dettmer, January 6, 2015, The Daily Beast, http://www.thedailybeast.com/articles/2014/11/06/spies-warned-white-house-don-t-hit-al-qaeda-in-syria.html

41 "After Foley Murder, More Jihadi Threats to Murder Hostages," by Nicholas Blandford, August 24, 2014, Christian Science Monitor, http://www.csmonitor.com/World/Middle-

East/2014/0824/After-Foley-murder-more-jihadi-threats-to-murder-hostages; AND "Qatar Ends Mediation for Arsal Hostages," by Middle East Eye and Agencies, December 8, 2014, http://www.middleeasteye.net/news/qatar-ends-mediation-lebanese-hostages-abducted-arsal-631606875

42 "Islamic State Kidnaps 3 Lebanese Men in Arsal," Naharnet, January 21, 2015, http://www.naharnet.com/stories/en/163843-islamic-state-kidnaps-3-lebanese-men-in-arsal

43 "AQAP Expresses Solidarity with 'Muslim Brothers' in Iraq Amidst US Airstrikes, Threatens US," by SITE staff, SITE Intelligence Group INSITE BLOG, August 14, 2014, http://news.siteintelgroup.com/blog/?view=entry&id=230

44 "Al Qaeda in Yemen Rebukes ISIS," by Paul Cruickshank, November 21, 2014, CNN, http://edition.cnn.com/2014/11/21/world/meast/al-qaeda-yemen-isis

45 "Al Qaeda in Yemen Rebukes ISIS," by Paul Cruickshank, November 21, 2014, CNN, http://edition.cnn.com/2014/11/21/world/meast/al-qaeda-yemen-isis

46 "Al-Wala' Wa'l-Bara' According to the 'Aqeedah of the Salaf," by Shaykh Muhammad Saeed al-Qahtani

47 Personal communications, January 19, 2012, Dr. (Col.) Eitan Azani, Deputy Dean, International Institute for Counter-Terrorism, IDC Herzliya

48 The FBI and U.S. Department of Homeland Security reportedly issued a bulletin to law enforcement stating that the Paris attacks demonstrate "a degree of sophistication and training traditionally not seen in recent small armed attacks." "France: Raids Kill 3 Suspects, Including 2 Wanted in Charlie Hebdo Attack," by Grego Bothelho, Ray Sanchez, and contributing CNN reporters, January 21, 2015, CNN, http://edition.cnn.com/2015/01/09/europe/charlie-hebdo-paris-shooting/index.html

49 "In Video, Coulibaly Says He Coordinated With Hebdo Shooters," by Jamie Dettmer, January 11, 2015, The Daily Beast, http://www.thedailybeast.com/articles/2015/01/11/in-video-coulibaly-says-he-coordinated-with-hebdo-shooters.html

50 The Charlie Hebdo attack left 12 victims dead, and the two gunmen died during a police siege at a factory near Dammartin-en-Goelle.

51 The kosher supermarket attack left 4 victims and the gunman dead; this same gunman killed the policewoman earlier.

52 "Video Shows Terrorist Responsible for Paris Market Attack Pledging Allegiance to Islamic State," by Thomas Joscelyn, January 11, 2015, The Long War Journal, http://www.longwarjournal.org/archives/2015/01/video_shows_terroris.php

53 Evidence has not emerged indicating that Amedy Coulibaly ever traveled to Iraq or Syria for IS training, or that he received support from this group to carry out the supermarket attack. "1st Charges Expected Over France Terror Attacks," January 20, 2015, CBS and Associate Press, http://www.cbsnews.com/news/france-charge-suspects-terror-attacks-links-kosher-store-killer-amedy-coulibaly

54 "France: Raids Kill 3 Suspects, Including 2 Wanted in Charlie Hebdo Attack," by Grego Bothelho, Ray Sanchez, and contributing CNN reporters, January 21, 2015, CNN, http://edition.cnn.com/2015/01/09/europe/charlie-hebdo-paris-shooting/index.html

55 "Belgian Arms Dealer Confesses to Supply Paris Attackers," by Shlomo Pariblat, January 14, 2015, Haaretz, http://www.cbsnews.com/news/france-charge-suspects-terror-attacks-links-kosher-store-killer-amedy-coulibaly

56 Also, Said, the elder of the Kouachi brothers, reportedly received weapons training and worked with AQAP in Yemen in 2011. "In Video, Coulibaly Says He Coordinated With Hebdo Shooters," by Jamie Dettmer, January 11, 2015, The Daily Beast, http://www.thedailybeast.com/articles/2015/01/11/in-video-coulibaly-says-he-coordinated-with-hebdo-shooters.html; AND "France: Raids Kill 3 Suspects, Including 2 Wanted in Charlie Hebdo Attack," by Grego Bothelho, Ray Sanchez, and contributing CNN reporters, January 21, 2015, CNN, http://edition.cnn.com/2015/01/09/europe/charlie-hebdo-paris-shooting/index.html

57 AQAP commander Nasr Ibn Ali al-Ansi claimed credit for the magazine attack on behalf of his group in a video message, and said that the late U.S.-born Muslim cleric, Anwar al-Awlaki, masterminded the operation before his death in 2011. He claimed that the attack was years in the making and conceived as revenge for Charlie Hebdo's depictions of the Islamic prophet, Muhammad. A man claiming to be the younger of the Kouachi brothers, Cherif, told CNN affiliate BFMTV that he was sent by AQAP to carry out the magazine massacre and that the late al-Awlaki financed his trip. "Al Qaeda Branch Claims Charlie Hebdo Attack Was Years in the Making," by Catherine E. Shoichet and Josh Levs, January 15, 2015, CNN, http://edition.cnn.com/2015/01/14/europe/charlie-hebdo-france-attacks; AND "Following the Tangled and Treacherous Trail After France Terror Attack," by Mariano Castillo, January 15, 2015, CNN, http://www.cnn.com/2015/01/13/europe/france-charlie-hebdo-attack-trail; AND "France: Raids Kill 3 Suspects, Including 2 Wanted in Charlie Hebdo Attack," by Grego Bothelho, Ray Sanchez, and contributing CNN reporters, January 21, 2015, CNN, http://edition.cnn.com/2015/01/09/europe/charlie-hebdo-paris-shooting/index.html

58 "New Details on Paris Terror Attack Suspects' Movements," January 15, 2015, CBS News and Associated Press, http://www.cbsnews.com/news/new-details-on-paris-terror-attack-suspects-movements

59 "Massive Search for Woman Suspected in Paris Hostage-Taking," by Michael Martinez, January 9, 2015, CNN, http://www.cnn.com/2015/01/09/world/france-woman-suspect

60 "Following the Tangled and Treacherous Trail After France Terror Attack," by Mariano Castillo, January 15, 2015, CNN, http://www.cnn.com/2015/01/13/europe/france-charlie-hebdo-attack-trail

61 Hayat Boumeddiene's last recorded call from her Turkish cell phone reportedly came on January 10, 2015 from Tel Abyad, an IS-controlled town next to the Akcakale crossing, where nearby residents say that IS informants are present on the Turkish side of the border. The Syrian side of the border crossing is under IS-control. From Tel Abyad, Boumeddiene is able to reach Raqqa by car in two hours. Raqqa is the IS stronghold city in Syria. "Paris Terror Attacks: Jihadi Killer's Widow in Syrian Terror Town," by Dominic Kennedy, January 12, 2015, The Australian, http://www.theaustralian.com.au/news/world/paris-terror-attacks-jihadi-killers-widow-in-syrian-terror-town/story-fnb64oi6-1227181998642?nk=ed2890e6718053ca2f762adf97c9364c

62 "1st Charges Expected Over France Terror Attacks," January 20, 2015, CBS and Associate Press, http://www.cbsnews.com/news/france-charge-suspects-terror-attacks-links-kosher-store-killer-amedy-coulibaly

63 "IS Spokesman Calls on Muslims in the West to Carry Out More Attacks Against 'Crusaders,' " by Bassem Mroue and Associated Press, January 26, 2016, U.S. News and World Report, http://www.usnews.com/news/world/articles/2015/01/26/is-spokesman-calls-on-muslims-in-west-to-commit-more-attacks; AND "Islamic State Calls on Muslims to Attack West," Associate Press and Military Times, January 26, 2015, http://www.militarytimes.com/story/military/pentagon/2015/01/26/islamic-state-calls-on-muslims-to-attack-west/22348047

64 "Coalitions Between Terrorist Organizations: Revolutionaries, Nationalists, and Islamists," by Ely Karmon, 2005, Leiden, The Netherlands: Martinus Nijhoff and VSP

65 "Allying to Kill: Terrorist Intergroup Cooperation and the Consequences for Lethality," by Michael C. Horowitz and Philip B. K. Potter, October 2013, Journal of Conflict Resolution, pages 1-27, http://dx/doi.org//10.1177/0022002712468726

66 "The Protean Enemy," by Jessica Stern, July/August 2003, Foreign Affairs, 82 (4), pages 27-40, http://www.foreignaffairs.com/articles/58995/jessica-stern/the-protean-enemy

67 "Fast Facts: The Embassy Bombings in Kenya and Tanzania," from the CNN Library, updated October 6, 2013, accessed January 26, 2015, CNN, http://www.cnn.com/2013/10/06/world/africa/africa-embassy-bombings-fast-facts

68 "The Real Threat from the Islamic State is to Muslims, Not the West," by Sunny Hundal, August 25, 2014, AlJazeera, http://www.aljazeera.com/indepth/opinion/2014/08/real-threat-from-islamic-state--201482316357532975.html

69 "The Terrorist Bureaucracy: Inside the Files of the Islamic State in Iraq," by Jacob N. Shapiro and Danielle F. Jung, The Boston Globe, December 14, 2014, http://www.bostonglobe.com/ideas/2014/12/14/the-terrorist-bureaucracy-inside-files-islamic-state-iraq/QtRMOARRYows0D18faA2FP/story.html

70 "Backgrounder: Islamic State in Iraq and Syria," by Zachary Laub and Jonathan Masters, August 8, 2014, Council on Foreign Relations, http://www.cfr.org/iraq/islamic-state-iraq-syria/p14811

71 Bill Roggio, "US Adds Harakat-ul-Mujahideen's Emir to Terrorism List," September 30, 2014, The Long War Journal, http://defenddemocracy.org/media-hit/bill-roggio-us-adds-harakat-ul-mujahideens-emir-to-terrorism-list

72 "Al-Qa'ida Central and Local Affiliates" by Vahid Brown in Assaf Moghadam and Brian Fishman (editors), Self Inflicted Wounds: Debates and Divisions Within Al-Qa'ida and its Periphery, pages 69-99, December 16, 2010, Combating Terrorism Center at West Point, https://www.ctc.usma.edu/v2/wp-content/uploads/2011/05/Self-Inflicted-Wounds.pdf; AND "The Al-Qaeda Nebula," in Beyond Al-Qaeda: The Global Jihadist Movement, 1st Edition, pages 73-80, document number MG-429-AF, 2006, by Angel Rabasa, Peter Chalk, Kim Cragin, Sara A. Daly, Heather S. Gregg, Theodore W. Karasik, Kevin A. O'Brien, and William Rosenau, RAND Corporation, http://www.rand.org/pubs/monographs/MG429.html

73 Black's Law Dictionary: Definitions of the Terms and Phrases of American and English Jurisprudence, Ancient and Modern, by Henry Cambell Black; Fifth Edition by The Publisher's Editorial Staff, contributing authors Joseph R. Nolan and M. J. Connolly, West Publishing Company, St. Paul Minnesota, 1979

74 Don Rassler and Vahid Brown, July 13, 2011, "The Haqqani Nexus and the Evolution of Al-Qa'ida," The Combating Terrorism Center at West Point, http://www.ctc.usma.edu/wp-content/uploads/2011/07/CTC-Haqqani-Report_Rassler-Brown-Final_Web.pdf

75 Tushar Ranjan Mohanty, "TTP: Hardening Lines," September 15, 2014, South Asia Intelligence Review, http://www.satp.org/satporgtp/sair/Archives/sair13/13_11.htm#assessment1

76 From September 2014 on out, varying media accounts ranged from reporting that the Pakistani Taliban and several of its leaders switched allegiance to IS and were sending fighters to Iraq and to Syria to help establish a caliphate, to a TTP denial of any pledge of allegiance to IS and a clarification that TTP faction leader Mullah Fazlullah's expression of support for IS was misinterpreted and that the Pakistani Taliban still considers Omar its

head and the group's members will continue following him. For instance: Amaud de Borchgrave, "Pakistan's Leader Wants ISIS to Succeed," September 24, 2014, Newsmax, http://www.newsmax.com/deBorchgrave/Pakistan-Leader-ISIS-TTP/2014/09/24/id/596667; AND Sajjad Hussain, "Pakistan Taliban Ditch Qaeda to Help ISIS," October 6, 2014, The Asian Age, http://www.asianage.com/print/334679; AND Press Trust of India, "Pakistani Taliban Denies Allegiance to Islamic State," updated October 7, 2014, ZeeNews of India, http://zeenews.india.com/news/south-asia/pakistani-taliban-denies-allegiance-to-islamic-state_1481227.html; AND Jacob Zenn, "Islamic State Finds New Ally in Pakistan's TTP," October 10, 2014, Vol. XII, No. 19, http://www.jamestown.org/uploads/media/TerrorismMonitorVol12Issue19_04.pdf; AND Dalit Halevy and Tova Dvorin, "Five Taliban Leaders Declare Loyalty to ISIS," October 14, 2014, Arutz Sheva, http://www.israelnationalnews.com/News/News.aspx/186141#.VD0pxCjzj6k

77 After his defection from the Pakistani Taliban, spokesman, Shahidullah Shahid, on October 13, 2014, reportedly pledged allegiance to al-Baghadadi on behalf of himself and five other emirs from the terrorist coalition who are also defectors. However, a week earlier, on October 6, 2014, the spokesman denied that the Pakistani Taliban had sworn allegiance to al-Baghdadi and IS. Bill Roggio and Thomas Joscelyn, "Discord Dissolves Pakistani Taliban Coalition," October 18, 2014, The Long War Journal, retrieved from http://defenddemocracy.org/media-hit/bill-roggio-discord-dissolves-pakistani-taliban-coalition

78 "Pakistani Taliban Splinter Group Again Pledges Allegiance to Islamic State," by The Long War Journal Staff, January 13, 2015, The Long War Journal, http://www.longwarjournal.org/archives/2015/01/video_pakistani_tali_2.php?utm_source =feedburner&utm_medium=email&utm_campaign=Feed%3A+LongWarJournalSiteWide+% 28The+Long+War+Journal+%28Site-Wide%29%29

79 Indicated by mild temperatures and a lack of snow cover on the mountains in what The Long War Journal assessed was western Pakistan.

80 The IS' reference to a Khorasan Shura echoes AQ's so-called Khorasan Shura, which is based in Syria. It is unclear if this indicates a split for AQ or if the two groups are using the same term because of its historical and apocalyptic underpinnings. According to Encyclopaedia Britannica, Khorasan is a reference to the historical region and realm comprising vast territory now in northeastern Iran, southern Turkmenistan, and northern Afghanistan. There are several ahadith that refer to Khorasan. Here are two: "Abu Hurairah narrated that the Messenger of Allah (s.a.w.) said: 'Black standards will come from Khurasan, nothing shall turn them back until they are planted in Jerusalem.' " Jami at-Tirmidhi, Vol 4, Book 7, Hadith 2269; AND "It was narrated that Abu Bakr Siddiq said: 'The Messenger of Allah (saw) told us:

"Dajjal [Antichrist] will emerge in a land in the east called Khorasan, and will be followed by people with faces like hammered shields." ' " Sunan Ibn Majah, Vol. 5, Book 36, Hadith 4072

81 "Islamic State Appoints Leaders of 'Khorasan Province,' Issues Veiled Threat to Afghan Taliban," by The Long War Journal staff, January 26, 2015, The Long War Journal, http://www.cnn.com/2015/01/25/africa/nigeria-boko-haram-battle-maiduguri

82 "Pakistani Taliban Splinter Group Again Pledges Allegiance to Islamic State," by The Long War Journal Staff, January 13, 2015, The Long War Journal, http://www.longwarjournal.org/archives/2015/01/video_pakistani_tali_2.php?utm_source =feedburner&utm_medium=email&utm_campaign=Feed%3A+LongWarJournalSiteWide+% 28The+Long+War+Journal+%28Site-Wide%29%29

83 The JuA comprised TTP factions from several tribal areas and districts.

84 Sajjad Tarakzai and Associated Foreign Press News, "New Taliban Group Vows Attacks in Pakistan," August 28, 2014, https://sg.news.yahoo.com/taliban-group-vows-attacks-pakistan-183650270.html

85 Bill Roggio, "Taliban Splinter Group Jamaat-ul-Ahrar Forms in Northwestern Pakistan," August 26, 2014, The Long War Journal, http://www.longwarjournal.org/archives/2014/08/taliban_splinter_gro.php

86 J. Caravelli, "Beyond sand and oil: The nuclear Middle East", e-book version, 2011, http://dx.doi.org/EISBN: 978-0-313-38706-7

87 J. Goldberg and M. Ambinder, "The ally from Hell," October 28, 2011, The Atlantic, http://www.theatlantic.com/magazine/archive/2011/12/the-ally-from-hell/308730/?single_page=true; AND R. Kazi, "Nuclear terrorism: The new terror of the 21st Century," 2013, Institute for Defence Studies & Analyses Monograph No. 27, http://www.idsa.in/system/files/Monograph27.pdf

88 Amaud de Borchgrave, "Pakistan's Leader Wants ISIS to Succeed," September 24, 2014, Newsmax, http://www.newsmax.com/deBorchgrave/Pakistan-Leader-ISIS-TTP/2014/09/24/id/596667; AND Jahan Zeb, "The Pashtun Land – Khyber Pakhtunkhwa, FATA, Afghanistan, Pakistan," April 5, 2012, AfPak Peace & Conflict Monitor, http://pdc-afpak.blogspot.com/2012/04/pashtun-land-khyber-pakhtunkhwa-fata.html

89 J. Scholfield and M. Zekulin, "Appraising the threat of an Islamist military coup in post-OBL Pakistan," 2011, Defense & Security Analysis, Vol. 27, Issue 4, 311-324. doi:10.1080/14751798.2011.632247; AND M. Tkacik, "Pakistan's Nuclear Weapons Program and Implications for US National Security," Vol. 24, Issue 2, 175-217, doi:10.1177/0047117809366202

90 J. Scholfield and M. Zekulin, "Appraising the threat of an Islamist military coup in post-OBL Pakistan," 2011, Defense & Security Analysis, Vol. 27, Issue 4, 311-324. doi:10.1080/14751798.2011.632247

91 The current crisis reportedly began on October 3, 2014, and was started by Pakistan repeatedly violating the Ceasefire Agreement in the worst breach of the truce since November 2003. Media reports indicate that Islamabad was evacuating civilians from forward areas on the Pakistani side of the International Border before launching military strikes against civilian populations on the Indian side. Among the possible motives floated: Pakistan was thought to be diverting public attention away from internal crises that include mounting violent demonstrations against the civilian government, whose relationship with the military deteriorated sharply; and the filing of a murder case against Prime Minister Sharif, his brother and Punjab Chief Minister, Shahbaz Sharif, and other officials over the death of two persons during an August 2014 clash between police and anti-government protestors. Ajai Sahni and Anurag Tripathi, "Mindless Adventurism," October 13, 2014, South Asia Intelligence Review, Vol. 13, No. 15, http://www.satp.org/satporgtp/sair/Archives/sair13/13_15.htm

92 News Briefs, October 6-12, 2014, South Asia Intelligence Review, Vol. 13, No. 15, http://www.satp.org/satporgtp/sair/Archives/sair13/13_15.htm

93 Ryan Mauro, "Al Qaeda Announces New Branch and Bid for Own Caliphate," The Clarion Project, September 4, 2014, http://www.clarionproject.org/analysis/al-qaeda-announces-new-branch-and-bid-own-caliphate

94 AQ's internal rift has only deepened since April 2013, a result of al-Baghdadi sidestepping al-Zawahiri, and the former eventually forging ahead with a self-styled caliphate project. Jihadi Websites Monitoring Group, "Summary of Information on Jihadist Websites," bimonthly report, first half of June 2014, published October 19, 2014, http://www.ict.org.il/Article/1232/Periodical_Review_Summary_from_the_Jihadi_Forums_The_First_Half_of_June_2014.

95 Of 178 states examined for the 2013 and 2014 Fragile State Index years, the #1 slot – the least stable state – for 2013 was held by Somalia; in 2014, South Sudan held the position. A Fragile States Index Year reflects data collected from the year before, so 2014 scores are based on data collected from January 1, 2013 to December 31, 2013, and so forth. Fund For Peace, Fragile States Index 2014, http://ffp.statesindex.org

96 Mark Mazzetti and Eric Schmitt, "In a Shift, Obama Extends U.S. Role in Afghan Combat," November 21, 2014, http://www.nytimes.com/2014/11/22/us/politics/in-secret-obama-extends-us-role-in-afghan-combat.html?_r=0

97 "Pakistan: Prevailing Internal Situation and its Implications for India," August 13, 2014 seminar report, remarks by Col. HPS Hansi, senior fellow, Centre for Land Warfare Studies, New Dehli, http://www.claws.in/images/events/pdf/1963726188_Report_Situation_in_Pakistan_13_August.pdf

98 The United Nations reports that Karachi is the 12th most populated urban settlement in the world, according to population size and ranking of urban agglomerations with more than 5 million inhabitants as of July 1, 2014. Note: The report, which studies the trends in urbanization, is based on national statistics that include primarily population census, but also estimates obtained from population registers or administrative statistics. The UN notes the heterogeneity of the urban definition across countries. The Population Division endeavored to use data or estimates based on the concept of urban agglomeration. UNICEF defines Urban Agglomeration as follows: "The population of a built-up or densely populated area containing the city proper, suburbs and continuously settled commuter areas of adjoining territory inhabited at urban levels of residential density." Sources: "World Urbanization Prospects: The 2014 Revision," United Nations, http://esa.un.org/unpd/wup/Highlights/WUP2014-Highlights.pdf; AND "Definitions," UNICEF, http://www.unicef.org/sowc2012/pdfs/SOWC-2012-DEFINITIONS.pdf

99 Among other resource avenues, IS derives income from extortion and smuggling operations, and from numerous captured oil and gas fields in Syria and Iraq. John C. K. Daly, "The Islamic State's Oil Network," October 10, 2014, Terrorism Monitor, Vol. XII, No. 19, http://www.jamestown.org/uploads/media/TerrorismMonitorVol12Issue19_04.pdf

100 Farhan Zahid, "The Caliphate in South Asia: A Profile of Hizb-ut Tahrir in Pakistan," Terrorism Monitor, Vol. 12, Issue 14, July 10, 2014, http://www.jamestown.org/programs/tm/single/?tx_ttnews%5Btt_news%5D=42600&tx_ttnews%5BbackPid%5D=757&no_cache=1#.VA6LDSjzj6k

101 For a historical snapshot of the Khilafa, see Edward N. Luttwak, "Caliphate Redivivus? Why a Careful Look at the 7th Century Can Predict How the New Caliphate Will End," August 1, 2014, Hoover Institution, http://www.hoover.org/research/caliphate-redivivus-why-careful-look-7th-century-can-predict-how-new-caliphate-will-end

102 Ariel Cohen, "Hizb ut-Tahrir: An Emerging Threat to U.S. Interests in Central Asia," May 30, 2003, The Heritage Foundation, http://www.heritage.org/research/reports/2003/05/hizb-ut-tahrir-an-emerging-threat-to-us-interests-in-central-asia

103 For example, see "An Explanatory Memorandum On the General Strategic Goal for the Group in North America," May 22, 1991, http://www.investigativeproject.org/documents/misc/20.pdf

104 See, "The Constitution of the Shia Imami Ismaili Muslims"
http://ismaili.net/Source/extra1.html

105 Hawalas are alternative banking systems that deal on a cash basis, making monies moving through them difficult or impossible to trace. Because they offer users anonymity, they are well used by terrorist organizations. Hawalas are particularly popular in many third world countries, and in the Islamic world.

106 At its core, the da'wa is the invitation to Islam targeting non-Muslims; and it can also function as a call to arms against a perceived enemy.

107 Associated Foreign Press, "Nigerian Town Seized by Boko Haram 'Part of Islamic Caliphate' Leader Says," August 24, 2014, The Telegraph, http://www.telegraph.co.uk/news/worldnews/africaandindianocean/nigeria/11054219/Nigerian-town-seized-by-Boko-Haram-part-of-Islamic-caliphate-leader-says.html

108 Stoyan Zaimov, "Boko Haram Declares 'Islamic Caliphate' in Captured Christian Town in Nigeria," August 25, 2014, The Christian Post, http://www.christianpost.com/news/boko-haram-declares-islamic-caliphate-in-captured-christian-town-in-nigeria-125293

109 Jacob Zenn, "Boko Haram: Recruitment, Financing, and Arms Trafficking in the Lake Chad Region," October 2014, CTC Sentinel, Vol. 7, Issue 10, https://www.ctc.usma.edu/v2/wp-content/uploads/2014/10/CTCSentinel-Vol7Iss103.pdf

110 During its seizures, Boko Haram continues rounding up and killing hundreds of civilians at a time, and generating waves of displaced persons who are resultantly facing starvation. African Armed Forces Journal, "Nigerian State Capital Surrounded by Boko Haram, September 12, 2014, http://www.aafonline.co.za/news/nigerian-state-capital-surrounded-boko-haram

111 During 2014, Boko Haram targeted Christian areas for slaughter and arson attacks in communities in Chibok and Biu local government areas of Borno State, including Chikwarkir; Gwozo; Izghe where at least 121 were killed; Karagau; Kautikabi; Kwada where five churches were ambushed and torched; Gamboru Ngala where up to 300 were killed in an attack; and Ngurotina. Boko Haram promised that there would be more such attacks. Numerous news reports, as well as reports from witnesses and local Christian leaders, confirmed by local, state, and federal authorities, inform that the terrorist group storms into the targeted villages, and its operative open fire on residents and hurl explosives into homes and in churches during services. The operatives also reportedly go house-to-house in search of their victims, and kill them by shooting them, hacking them with machetes, and slitting their throats. Those trying to escape become prey as they are hunted down and killed in the surrounding bush-land. Boko Haram has even returned to the same attack scene, such as it

did in Kautikari, to kill villagers who remain in the area. Military response is reportedly slow, and there have been allegations that the military has ignored distress calls, and has even failed to show up at an attack scene. Consequently, the terrorist group has been taking hours to go though the villages to make sure the carnage is massive and the villages are torched, carting off the foodstuffs and domestic animals that its operatives round up during the attacks. The group has an operational camp in the Sambisa Forest from which it launches attacks. Pastor Luka Bitrus, whose entire church was displaced due to an attack nearby the forest, in Gwoza, on December 18, 2012, referred to his EYN congregation of Sasawa village, Gwoza, as "a remnant of a church in exile." He said Boko Haram returned to attack area communities repeatedly. There is nothing new under the sun. Christian Solidarity Worldwide Chief Executive Mervyn Thomas in July 2014 called the recent attacks particularly in Borno State "... tantamount to religious cleansing ... " and said that it violates the right to freedom of religion or belief "as enshrined in article 38 of Nigeria's federal constitution." He renewed calls for effective protection of civilians, particularly in southern Borno and southern Kaduna "so they can go about their daily lives without the threat of violence or death." Sources: "The Strategic Limitations of Boko Haram in Southern Nigeria," by Jacob Zenn, August 2012, Combating Terrorism Center Sentinel, Vol. 5, Issue 8, Combating Terrorism Center at West Point, https://www.ctc.usma.edu/v2/wp-content/uploads/2012/08/CTCSentinel-Vol5Iss86.pdf; AND National Consortium for the Study of Terrorism and Responses to Terrorism, Background Report: "Boko Haram Recent Attacks," May 2014, http://www.start.umd.edu/pubs/STARTBackgroundReport_BokoHaramRecentAttacks_May 2014_0.pdf; AND "Nigeria's Boko Haram 'in Village Massacre,' " February 16, 2014, BBC News, http://www.bbc.com/news/world-africa-26220300; AND "Boko Haram Islamists Massacre Christian Villagers in Borno State, Nigeria," February 17, 2014, Morning Star News, http://morningstarnews.org/2014/02/boko-haram-islamists-massacre-christian-villagers-in-borno-state-nigeria; AND "Boko Haram Burns Churches, Kills More Than 30 People, Residents Say," by Aminu Abubakar, June 29, 2014, CNN, http://www.cnn.com/2014/06/29/world/africa/nigeria-boko-haram-violence; AND "Nigeria: 'Boko Haram' Attack Villages Near Chibok," June 29, 2014, BBC News, http://www.bbc.com/news/world-africa-28080030?print=true; AND "Nigeria: Chibok Burns Again – As Gunmen Kill 51, Burn Churches, Houses," by Henry Umoru and Ndahi Marama, June 30, 2014, AllAfrica, http://allafrica.com/stories/201406300466.html; AND "Boko Haram Attacks Churches in Nigeria, 50 Killed," Associated Foreign Press, June 30, 2014, The Times of India, http://timesofindia.indiatimes.com/world/rest-of-world/Boko-Haram-attacks-churches-in-nigeria-50-killed/articleshow/37526767.cms; AND "Nigeria: Breakthrough in Chibok Abductions After Week Marked by Violence," Christian Solidarity Worldwide USA, July 1, 2014, http://dynamic.csw.org.uk/article.asp?t=press&id=1733; AND

"Boko Haram Declares 'Islamic Caliphate' in Captured Christian Town in Nigeria," by Stoyan Zaimov, August 25, 2014, The Christian Post, http://www.christianpost.com/news/boko-haram-declares-islamic-caliphate-in-captured-christian-town-in-nigeria-125293; AND "Boko Haram Kills 15 in Northeast Nigerian Town: Witnesses," by Lanre Ola, December 30, 2014, Reuters, http://www.reuters.com/article/2014/12/30/us-nigeria-violence-idUSKBN0K814K20141230; AND "Seven Boko Haram Terrorists Die as their Bomb Detonates Enroute to Their Target," December 31, 2014, Nigeria Watch, http://www.nigerianwatch.com/news/6090-seven-boko-haram-terrorists-die-as-their-bomb-detonates-enroute-to-their-target

112 In July 2014, Human Rights Watch reported that Boko Haram slaughtered more than 2,053 civilians during the first half of 2014. Africa Check, a fact-checking project of the AFP, in partnership with the Journalism Department of Witwatersrand, South Africa, reports that the October 2014 claim of Nigeria's President, Goodluck Johathan, that more than 13,000 people have been killed in the Boko Haram insurgency, is "broadly correct." Researcher Tolu Ogunlesi of Africa Check concluded: "The available data suggests that as few [sic] 9,000 and as many as 17,500 people have died in the insurgency. The latter figure includes killings by both Boko Haram and the Nigerian military." He noted that the group began its insurgency in 2009. Sources: Human Rights Watch, "Nigeria: Boko Haram Kills 2,053 Civilians in 6 Months – Apparent Crimes Against Humanity," July 15, 2014, http://www.hrw.org/news/2014/07/15/nigeria-boko-haram-kills-2053-civilians-6-months; AND Africa Check, "Have Over 13,000 People Been Killed in Nigeria's Insurgency? The Claim is Broadly Correct," by Tolu Ogunlesi, October 14, 2014, http://africacheck.org/reports/have-13000-people-been-killed-in-nigerias-insurgency-the-claim-is-broadly-correct

113 "10 Killed, Four Churches Burned in Nigeria – Boko Haram Suspected in Rampage in Predominantly Christian Area," by Lekan Otufodunrin, December 6, 2012, WorldWatch Monitor, https://www.worldwatchmonitor.org/2012/12-December/article_1951963.html

114 "Nigeria Elections Put Christians in Danger of More Muslim Attacks," by Cheryl Wetzstein, January 27, 2015, The Washington Times, http://www.washingtontimes.com/news/2015/jan/27/nigeria-elections-put-christians-in-danger-of-more/

115 Boko Haram militants, from January 3-5, 2015, launched raids in and around the fishing settlement of Baga on the shores of Lake Chad in Nigeria's northeastern Borno State, where the group has a heavy footprint. The group overpowered and set fire to the Multinational Joint Task Force base in Doro Gowon where Nigeria, Chad, Niger, Cameroon, and Benin cooperate in counterterrorism operations, and set the soldiers to flight, which left area residents defenseless. Townspeople in 16 surrounding villages were targeted for arson

attacks and firepower from assault rifles and rocket-propelled grenades. Early human death toll estimates range from 150 to 2,000, according to local government, political, and military officials, and NGOs including Human Rights Watch and Amnesty International. Newsweek noted that if accurate, the reports would mean that up to a fifth of Baga's population of 10,000 has been killed. Thousands fled the area, with some drowning in the lake as their boats capsized, and as they tried to swim to safety to a nearby mosquito-infested island lacking sources of food. Satellite imagery obtained by Human Rights Watch captured images of the arson, which the group reported showed large-scale destruction to buildings and trees. The Washington Post noted an Associated Foreign Press (AFP) report informing that Boko Haram's attack means that the group controls all of Borno's borders with Niger, Chad, and Cameroon. Sources: "Boko Haram May Have Just Killed 2,000 People: 'Killing Went On and On and On,' " by Terry McCoy, January 9, 2015, The Washington Post, http://www.washingtonpost.com/news/morning-mix/wp/2015/01/09/boko-haram-may-have-killed-2000-people-in-one-attack; AND "Nigeria: Massacre Possibly Deadliest in Boko Haram's History," January 9, 2015, Amnesty International, http://www.amnesty.org/en/for-media/press-releases/nigeria-massacre-possibly-deadliest-boko-haram-s-history-2015-01-09-0; AND "Boko Haram Kill 2,000 People in One Town in Five Days, Say Officials," by Catherine Phillips, January 9, 2015, Newsweek, http://www.newsweek.com/boko-haram-kill-2000-people-one-town-five-days-298218; AND "2000 Feared Killed in 'Deadliest' Boko Haram Attack in Nigeria," by Aminu Abubakar and Faith Karimi, January 12, 2015, CNN, http://www.cnn.com/2015/01/09/africa/boko-haram-violence; AND "Boko Haram Crisis: Why it is Hard to Know the Truth in Nigeria," by Will Ross, BBC News, January 13, 2015, http://www.bbc.com/news/world-africa-30794829; AND Human Rights Watch, "Dispatches: What Really Happened in Baga, Nigeria?" by Mausi Segun, January 14, 2015, http://www.hrw.org/news/2015/01/14/dispatches-what-really-happened-baga-nigeria; AND "Boko Haram Continues to Slaughter Nigerians," by Laura Grossman, January 14, 2015, The Long War Journal, http://www.longwarjournal.org/archives/2015/01/boko_haram_attacks_c-print.php

116 African Armed Forces Journal, "New ISIS Strategy Threatens Africa," August 27, 2014, http://www.aafonline.co.za./new-isis-strategy-threatens-africa

117 "Strategic City Falls in Nigeria's Battle Against Boko Haram," by Aminu Abubakar, January 26, 2015, CNN, http://www.cnn.com/2015/01/25/africa/nigeria-boko-haram-battle-maiduguri

118 In addition to Gwoza, other captured territories in the Borno State alone include Baga, Bama, Banki, Damboa, Dikwa, Gamboru Ngala, Marte, and Madagali; and Boko Haram has surrounded the capital, Maiduguri. On January 10, 2015, Boko Haram sent a girl around 10 years old to her death in Maiduguri, where they strapped her with an explosive device, sent

her into a busy market, and detonated the explosives, killing at least 20 people and injuring scores of other victims. The insurgent group camps out in the Sambisa forest in this region, from which it launches many of its attacks. Sources: "Boko Haram Takes Cues from ISIS: Ferocious New Friends?" Robert Rotberg, September 10, 2014, Christian Science Monitor, http://www.csmonitor.com/World/Africa/Africa-Monitor/2014/0910/Boko-Haram-takes-cues-from-ISIS-Ferocious-new-friends; AND Associated Foreign Press, "Nigerian Troops Battle Boko Haram Pre-Dawn Raid," September 2, 2014, Africa Armed Forces journal, http://www.aafonline.co.za/news/nigerian-troops-battle-boko-haram-pre-dawn-raid; AND "Boko Haram Continues to Slaughter Nigerians," by Laura Grossman, January 14, 2015, The Long War Journal, http://www.longwarjournal.org/archives/2015/01/boko_haram_attacks_c-print.php

119 Encyclopaedia Britannica's Guide to Black History, "Slavery," accessed Sept. 4, 2014, http://www.britannica.com/blackhistory/article-24157

120 African Armed Forces journal, "Nigerian State Capital Surrounded by Boko Haram, September 12, 2014, http://www.aafonline.co.za/news/nigerian-state-capital-surrounded-boko-haram

121 Boko Haram uses Niger, Chad, and Cameroon as safe havens, for training purposes, as a transit point, for planning attacks, and for recruitment activities. Jacob Zenn, "Boko Haram's International Connections," January 14, 2013, Counter-terrorism Sentinel, Combating Terrorism Center at West Point, https://www.ctc.usma.edu/posts/boko-harams-international-connections

122 The warning came after repeated rounds of fighting between Boko Haram militants and Cameroonian troops. President Biya said in October 2014 that he would pursue the group "until it's totally wiped out." His country has been vocal in criticisms regarding the lack of coordinate multi-state response to Boko Haram's unbridled rampage. "Boko Haram Leader Threatens Cameroon in YouTube Video," Al Arabiya News, January 7, 2015, http://english.alarabiya.net/en/News/africa/2015/01/07/Boko-Haram-leader-threatens-Cameroon-in-YouTube-video-.html

123 Jacob Zenn, "Boko Haram's Radical Ideologue: An In-Depth Look at Northern Nigeria's Abu Shekau," August 31, 2011, Militant Leadership Monitor, Vol. 2, Issue 8, http://mlm.jamestown.org/single/?tx_ttnews%5Btt_news%5D=38358&tx_ttnews%5BbackPid%5D=567&no_cache=1#.VAeUpyjzj6k

124 Laura Grossman, "Boko Haram's New Caliphate," August 25, 2014, The Long War Journal, http://www.longwarjournal.org/archives/2014/08/boko_harams_new_cali-print.php

125 Boko Haram was referred to as the "Nigerian Taliban" by outsiders from 2003 to 2009. Jacob Zenn, "Boko Haram's International Connections," January 14, 2013, Counter-terrorism Sentinel, Combating Terrorism Center at West Point, https://www.ctc.usma.edu/posts/boko-harams-international-connections

126 The National Counterterrorism Center, "Boko Haram," Counterterrorism 2014 Calendar, http://www.nctc.gov/site/groups/boko_haram.html

127 The perceived apostate "unbeliever" governments that AQIM seeks to overthrow include Algeria, Libya, Mali, Mauritania, Morocco, and Tunisia. Terrorism Research & Analysis Consortium, "Al Qaeda in the Lands of the Islamic Maghreb (AQIM)," accessed October 29, 2014, http://www.trackingterrorism.org/group/al-qaeda-lands-islamic-maghreb-aqim-salafist-group-preaching-and-fighting-see-separate-entry

128 United Nations Security Council (UNSC) Al-Qaida and Taliban Sanctions Committee (1267) List, "The Organization of Al-Qaida in the Islamic Maghreb," updated September 9, 2014, http://www.un.org/sc/committees/1267/NSQE01401E.shtml; AND United Nations Security Council (UNSC) Al-Qaida and Taliban Sanctions Committee (1267) List, "Jama'atu Ahlis-Sunna Lidda'awati wal-jihad (Boko Haram)," updated September 9, 2014, http://www.un.org/sc/committees/1267/NSQE13814E.shtml; AND United States Department of State, "Al-Qa'ida in the Islamic Maghreb," April 2014, Country Reports on Terrorism 2013, Ch. 6, Foreign Terrorist Organizations, http://www.state.gov/j/ct/rls/crt/2013/224829.htm

129 The National Counterterrorism Center, "Boko Haram," Counterterrorism 2014 Calendar, http://www.nctc.gov/site/groups/boko_haram.html; AND United Nations Security Council (UNSC) Al-Qaida and Taliban Sanctions Committee (1267) List, "Jama'atu Ahlis-Sunna Lidda'awati wal-jihad (Boko Haram)," updated September 9, 2014, http://www.un.org/sc/committees/1267/NSQE13814E.shtml

130 Marc-Antoine Perouse de Montclos, "Nigeria's Interminable Insurgency? Addressing the Boko Haram Crisis," September 2014, Africa Program, Chatham House, http://www.chathamhouse.org/sites/files/chathamhouse/field/field_document/20140901 BokoHaramPerousedeMontclos_0.pdf

131 Jacob Zenn, "Boko Haram's International Connections," January 14, 2013, Counter-terrorism Sentinel, Combating Terrorism Center at West Point, https://www.ctc.usma.edu/posts/boko-harams-international-connections

132 Zachary Elkaim, "Boko Haram Leader Releases Video on Maiduguri Attack, Threatens US," December 13, 2013, The Long War Journal, http://www.longwarjournal.org/archives/2013/12/shekau_strikes_back-print.php

133 In November 2011, Associate Press reported that Boko Haram apparently split into three factions: the first group is "moderate" and wants to end the violence, the second wants a peace agreement, and the third refuses to negotiate and wants to implement strict Sharia law across Nigeria. Al Jazeera reported that the group split into a number of factions with differing aims, even with political links. Jon Gambrell, Associated Press, "Nigeria: Radical Muslim sect grows more dangerous, Nov. 4, 2011, http://news.yahoo.com/nigeria-radical-muslim-sect-grows-more-dangerous-164544895.html; Al Jazeera, "Profile: Boko Haram," updated May 18, 2013, http://www.aljazeera.com/news/africa/2012/01/20121974241393331.html

134 Laura Grossman, "Boko Haram's New Caliphate," August 25, 2014, The Long War Journal, http://www.longwarjournal.org/archives/2014/08/boko_harams_new_cali-print.php

135 Jacob Zenn, "Boko Haram's Radical Ideologue: An In-Depth Look at Northern Nigeria's Abu Shekau," August 31, 2011, Militant Leadership Monitor, Vol. 2, Issue 8, http://mlm.jamestown.org/single/?tx_ttnews%5Btt_news%5D=38358&tx_ttnews%5BbackPid%5D=567&no_cache=1#.VAeUpyjzj6k

136 Farouk Chothia, "Who are Nigeria's Boko Haram Islamists?" updated May 20, 2014, BBC News, http://www.bbc.com/news/world-africa-13809501?print=true; AND Marc-Antoine Perouse de Montclos, "Nigeria's Interminable Insurgency? Addressing the Boko Haram Crisis," September 2014, Africa Program, Chatham House, http://www.chathamhouse.org/sites/files/chathamhouse/field/field_document/20140901BokoHaramPerousedeMontclos_0.pdf

137 The Generous Quran, translated by Usama Dakdok

138 Genocide Watch, "Nigeria: Video from Boko Haram Shows Civilian Massacre," December 27, 2014, http://genocidewatch.net/2015/01/07/video-from-boko-haram-shows-civilian-massacre; AND "Boko Haram May Have Just Killed 2,000 People: 'Killing Went On and On and On,' " by Terry McCoy, January 9, 2015, The Washington Post, http://www.washingtonpost.com/news/morning-mix/wp/2015/01/09/boko-haram-may-have-killed-2000-people-in-one-attack

139 Formerly Ansar al-Sharia in Benghazi

140 Al-Arabia, "Benghazi Declared 'Islamic Emirate' by Militants," July 31, 2014, http://english.alarabiya.net/en/News/middle-east/2014/07/31/Libya-s-Ansar-al-Sharia-declares-Islamic-state-in-Benghazi.html

141 From Benghazi, sea routes include transit points at the Gulf of Bardi, Libya and the Gulf of Salloum, Egypt, with smaller boats moving the contraband between these two points, and with the town of Salloum being a major site of weapons seizures; another key transit point is

the Port of Marsa Matrouh, Egypt, which facilitates moving the contraband into North Sinai. The bulk of trafficking occurs along five main land routes that begin in Benghazi, with two passing through Marsa Matrouh, two through the oasis city of Siwa, and another linking up with fishing boats moving the contraband from Marsa Matrouh to Northern Sinai; there is also significant activity between Salloum and its environs, and between this town and Marsa Matrough. Frederic Wehrey, David Bishop, and Ala' Alrababa'h, "Backdrop to an Intervention: Sources of Egyptian-Libyan Border Tension," September 11, 2014, International Relations and Security Network, ETH Zurich, http://www.isn.ethz.ch/Digital-Library/Articles/Detail/?ots591=4888caa0-b3db-1461-98b9-e20e7b9c13d4&lng=en&id=183360

142 Andrew McGregor, "Libya's Ansar al-Shari's Declares the Islamic Emirate of Benghazi," August 8, 2014, Terrorism Monitor, Vol. 12, No. 16, http://www.jamestown.org/single/?tx_ttnews%5Btt_news%5D=42729&tx_ttnews%5BbackPid%5D=7#.U-0e6Cjzj6n

143 A shura council is a traditional Islamic consultative body responsible for top decision-making and other key functions.

144 There are distinctions in Libya's complex web of militias, which oftentimes have overlapping, shifting, even contradictory state and non-state loyalties and alliances. Such distinctions are hardly reassuring for Westerners. Generally speaking, in the evolving landscape in Libya as it stands today in the post-Qaddafi period: Armed "Islamist" militias tend to have a political arm or linkage, and enjoy the legitimacy of state sponsorship to varying degrees, as well as different levels of backing – some quite robust – by local populations. They often function as "peacekeeping" brigades and units where the national army has a limited presence. "Jihadist" militias take a rejectionist stand toward the established state authority, although even they may enjoy some state backing due to gaps in state security, and their levels of popular support at this stage are somewhat weaker in comparison to "Islamist" militias. They are typically not open to compromise on religious matters and to non-violent participation in the political process. "Islamist" militias are inclined to morph into "jihadist" militias when developments do not proceed the way they expect and sharia is not implemented in full. We are likely to see more of the "Islamist"-to-"jihadist" militancy dynamic in Libya, which is socially conservative, as it citizens struggle with forces of modernization clashing with the fundamental precepts of Islam in the post-Qaddafi political space during their nation-building process, which is taking shape in a regional atmosphere where Salafia Jihadia and anti-Western sentiments are on the rise. The "Islamist" movement in Libya combines the Sufi tradition of the Sanussi Order with "strident" Salafism; and until 2011, "Islamist" ideas were shaped in exile in Western countries and banned by Colonel Qaddafi, according to Manal Omar, who was a member of

the Libya Stabilization Team under the National Transitional Council formed during Libya's 2011 revolution. She informed that the Sanussi Order was founded in Mecca in 1837, and was "austere but rejected fanaticism." According to Omar: "The so-called Sanussiyya movement was revivalist, bringing together the Sufi Islamic tradition and religious reforms that looked to the life of the Prophet Mohammed as a social model, which was also the original concept of Saudi Arabia's Wahhabism." The Sanussi Order spearheaded "the largest anticolonial campaign – a form of jihad" against the Italian presence in Libya in 1911, Omar informed, and on a later note of assurance said that 90% of Libyans are Sunni Muslims who follow the Maliki school of thought, which she described as "the more moderate of the four traditional schools of jurisprudence." The position of the four schools of Islamic jurisprudence on a sliding scale of "moderate" to "radical" can be argued, and oftentimes the distinctions are blurred, even deliberately so in order to meet particular Islamic objectives. What is important is that in all Islamic ages, all these four schools are in agreement that "defensive" jihad becomes Fard Ayn – a personal duty incumbent upon all Muslims, beginning with those whose land is "attacked" by the non-Muslims and extending outward to Muslims worldwide – until sufficient manpower and money are collected in the interest of "repelling an aggressor." In the post-9-11 age, where, in the interest of self-preservation, Western-led counter-terrorism operations extend into lands under Muslim control where most of the terrorism emanates, the proverbial line dividing Libya's "Islamist" militias from its "jihadist" militias is thin, indeed. As "strident" Salafism is stoked by the flames of Salafia Jihadia and by an influx of foreign jihadi fighters into Libya, the mystical aspects of the Sufi component of this country's "Islamist" movement are going up in smoke, and the forces of militancy are further entrenching themselves as they exploit the vulnerabilities in the delicate national transition process. As a result, militancy in Libya is spiking to dangerous levels that threaten regional and global security. Sources: Abdullah Azzam, "Defense of the Muslim Lands – The First Obligation After Iman," https://www.archive.org/stream/IslamicBooksByIbnTaymiyyahMaqdisiAndAbdullahAzzam/Defence_of_Muslim_Lands_Abdullah_Azzam_djvu.txt; AND Alison Pargeter, "Islamist Militant Groups in Post-Qadhafi Libya," February 2013, Combating Terrorism Center Sentinel, https://www.ctc.usma.edu/wp-content/uploads/2013/02/CTCSentinel-Vol6Iss21.pdf; AND Faisal Irshaid, "Profile: Libya's Ansar al-Sharia," updated June 13, 2014, BBC Monitoring, http://www.bbc.com/news/world-africa-27732589; AND Andrew McGregor, "Libya's Ansar al-Sharia Declares and Islamic Emirate of Benghazi, Aug. 8, 2014, Terrorism Monitor, Vol. 12, Issue 16, http://www.jamestown.org/programs/tm/single/?tx_ttnews%5Btt_news%5D=42729&tx_ttnews%5BbackPid%5D=757&no_cache=1#.VLK86ijzj6k; AND Manal Omar, "Libya: Rebuilding From Scratch," Woodrow Wilson Center, accessed January 15, 2015, http://www.wilsoncenter.org/islamists/libya-rebuilding-scratch

145 Many groups under this Islamist umbrella group sympathize with AQ; and are affiliated with the Muslim Brotherhood, which has a stronghold in Misrata. In addition to Ansar al-Sharia, two noteworthy groups among the Shura Council of Benghazi Revolutionaries include: (1) 17 February Brigade – (a) named after the anti-Qaddafi oppositional forces' February 17, 2011 Day of Rage modeled on Tunisia and Egypt events; (b) funded by Libya's Defense Ministry to provide de facto security in Benghazi; (c) believed to be the largest and best armed militia in Eastern Libya, made up of 12 battalions equipped with light and heavy weaponry (d) prior to the September 11, 2012 attack on the U.S. Special Mission and Annex in Benghazi, the U.S. employed this brigade to provide security at the compound; per the testimony of Gregory Hicks, Deputy Chief of Mission for the U.S. Embassy in Libya, the highest-ranking official in Libya at the time of the attack, elements of the 17 February Martyrs Brigade were complicit; the U.S. House Republicans released on April 23, 2013 a progress report on their investigation into this attack and implicated this brigade in the kidnapping of American citizens, and in the issuance of threats against U.S. military assets. (2) Libya Shield Brigade No. 1– (a) part of the National Shield, a national army in waiting; (b) Revolutionary brigades assigned control of the National Shield to the chief of the National Army, Maj. Gen. Yousef al-Mangoush, thus circumventing the National Army bureaucracy. National Shield top commander, Wissam Ben Hamid, former commander of the Benghazi-based Free Libya Martyrs during the uprising, and his ally, Muhammad al-Gharbi, who was head of the Rafallah al-Sahati brigade, met with U.S. Ambassador Chris Stevens two days before the latter was killed during the September 11, 2012 attack. They told Stevens to exercise "control" over Yousef, whom they were trying to push from power. Asharq Al-Awsat, "Gaddafi Ready for Libya's 'Day of Rage,' " February 9, 2011, http://www.aawsat.net/2011/02/article55247591/print; AND Small Arms Survey, "Armed Groups in Libya: Typology and Roles," June 2012, http://www.smallarmssurvey.org/fileadmin/docs/H-Research_Notes/SAS-Research-Note-18.pdf; AND Eli Lake, "Exclusive: Libya Cable Detailed Threats," October 8, 2012, http://www.thedailybeast.com/articles/2012/10/08/exclusive-libya-cable-detailed-threats.html; AND John Rosenthal, "Newsmax Exclusive: US Hired al-Qaida-Linked Group to Defend Benghazi Mission," May 3, 2013, Newmax, http://www.newsmax.com/Newsfront/benghazi-consulate-protected-alqaida/2013/05/02/id/502565; AND Committee on Oversight and Government Reform, House of Representatives, 113th Congress, 1st Session, "Benghazi: Exposing Failure and Recognizing Courage," May 8, 2013, Serial No 113-30, http://oversight.house.gov/wp-content/uploads/2014/02/2013-05-08-Ser.-No.-113-30-FC-Benghazi-Exposing-Failure-and-Recognizing-Courage.pdf; AND Jamie Dettmer, "Libyan Militias Shape Country's Future," May 24, 2013, The Jamestown Foundation, http://www.jamestown.org/regions/africa/single/?tx_ttnews%5Btt_news%5D=40922&tx_t

tnews%5BbackPid%5D=55&cHash=f4253060957ba4bf9d7a7d4eeb50c0c1#.UhEIWuAQ1bs ; AND Faisal Irshaid, "Profile: Libya's Ansar al-Sharia," updated June 13, 2014, BBC Monitoring, http://www.bbc.com/news/world-africa-27732589; AND Timothy Robinson, "Libya," Standard Note 06864, April 11, 2014, International Affairs and Defence, UK briefing papers, http://webcache.googleusercontent.com/search?q=cache:ClI5P4FNcsUJ:www.parliament.uk /briefing-papers; AND Andrew McGregor, "Libya's Ansar al-Shari's Declares the Islamic Emirate of Benghazi," August 8, 2014, Terrorism Monitor, Vol. 12, No. 16, http://www.jamestown.org/single/?tx_ttnews%5Btt_news%5D=42729&tx_ttnews%5Bback Pid%5D=7#.U-0e6Cjzj6n

146 Ludovico Carlino, "Profile of Libyan Terrorist Group Ansar al-Sharia – Ansar al-Shari'a: Transforming Libya into a Land of Jihad," Jan. 10, 2014, Terrorism Monitor, http://www.matthewaid.com/post/72882603307/profile-of-libyan-terrorist-group-ansar-al-sharia

147 Alison Pargeter, "Islamist Militant Groups in Post-Qadhafi Libya," CTC Sentinel, Combating Terrorism Center at West Point, Feb. 20, 2013, http://www.ctc.usma.edu/posts/islamist-militant-groups-in-post-qadhafi-libya

148 United States Department of State, Office of the Spokesperson, "Terrorist Designations of Three Ansar al-Shari'a Organizations and Leaders," January 10, 2014, http://www.state.gov/r/pa/prs/ps/2014/01/219519.htm

149 Ludovico Carlino, "Profile of Libyan Terrorist Group Ansar al-Sharia – Ansar al-Shari'a: Transforming Libya into a Land of Jihad," Jan. 10, 2014, Terrorism Monitor, http://www.matthewaid.com/post/72882603307/profile-of-libyan-terrorist-group-ansar-al-sharia

150 Federal Research Division, Library of Congress under an Interagency Agreement with the Combating Terrorism Technical Support Office's Irregular Warfare Support Program, "Al-Qaeda in Libya: A Profile," August 2012, http://fas.org/irp/world/para/aq-libya-loc.pdf

151 Aaron Y. Zelin, "Libya's jihadists beyond Benghazi," The Middle East Channel, Aug. 12, 2013, http://mideast.foreignpolicy.com/posts/2013/08/12/libyas_jihadists_beyond_benghazi

152 Synopsis of Abu Sufian Ibrahim Ahmed Hamouda bin Qumu: Hamouda is a citizen of Libya who goes by several aliases and has used a false Mauritanian passport. He is a former member of the Libyan Islamic Fighting Group (LIFG), an alleged member of AQ, and a member of the North African Extremist Network (NAEN). NAEN is a Tier 0 Counterterrorism Target because it poses a "clear and immediate danger" to US persons or interests, and LIFG is a Tier 1 Counterterrorism Target, which is defined as a terrorist group, especially one with

state support, that has demonstrated the intention and the capability to attack U.S. persons or interests. As an employee of the Wafa Humanitarian Organization (Al-Wafa) in Kabul, Afghanistan, he used the front organization for "extremist activities." The Libyan government stated that Hamouda has been accused of a number of crimes, among the murder, armed assault, and narcotics distribution. He escaped from prison while serving a 10-year sentence. Hamouda trained in Usama bin Laden's (UBL) Torkham Camp in Afghanistan, and fought in the Afghan war against the former Soviet Union. While living in Sudan, he worked for one of UBL's companies, Wadi Al-'Aqiq, driving a truck. As a member of LIFG, he was assigned to the military committee. He also told authorities that he lived in Peshawar, Pakistan, an area under tribal rather than governmental control, and a haunt for UBL. He disclosed tha he maintained radio contact with suspected militant elements in Afghanistan. Hamouda fought with the Talaban against the Northern Alliance. Another fellow detainee alleged that Hamouda assisted the Qadhafi Foundation in Peshawar, which relocated militants and their families. He was assessed as posing a medium to high risk threat against the U.S., its interests and allies. Hamouda has enduring ties with militants and long-term associations with AQ members, and with other jihadist groups. The Libyan government considers him a "dangerous man with no qualms about committing terrorist acts," and said that he was known as one of the militant commanders of the Afghan Arab Mujahideen, which formed as a nucleus in the AfPak area in the 1990s after the Soviet Jihad. Hamouda is considered to be of high intelligence value. He has a personality disorder. Source: A declassified assessment released on 22 April 2005 by the U.S. Department of Defense Joint Task Force Guantanamo Bay, which is archived on-line in "The Guantanamo Docket" compiled by The New York Times at http://projects.nytimes.com/guantanamo/detainees/557-abu-sufian-ibrahim-ahmed-hamuda-bin-qumu/documents/11

153 Africa Armed Forces journal, "Libya: Al Qaeda-Linked Group Leader Found Dead," April 9, 2014, http://www.aafonline.co.za/news/libya-al-qaeda-linked-group-leader-found-dead; AND TRAC, "Islamic Youth Shura Council," accessed August 17, 2014, http://www.trackingterrorism.org/group/islamic-youth-shura-council

154 HIS Jane's Intelligence Review, "Libyan Group's Pledge to Islamic State Raises Risk of Fighting Between Rival Islamist Group in Derna," October 6, 2014, http://www.janes.com/article/44182/libyan-group-s-pledge-to-islamic-state-raises-risk-of-fighting-between-rival-islamist-groups-in-derna; AND Aaron Y. Zelin, "The Islamic State's First Colony in Libya," October 10, 2014, The Washington Institute for Near East Policy, Policy Watch 2325, http://www.washingtoninstitute.org/policy-analysis/view/the-islamic-states-first-colony-in-libya

155 Aaron Y. Zelin, "The Islamic State's Archipelago of Provinces," November 14, 2014, The Washington Institute for Near East Policy, http://www.washingtoninstitute.org/policy-analysis/view/the-islamic-states-archipelago-of-provinces

156 Aya Elbrqawi and Essam Mohamed, "Is Derna Becoming an Islamist Emirate?" April 8, 2014, Magharebia, http://magharebia.com/en_GB/articles/awi/features/2014/04/08/feature-0; AND Africa Armed Forces Journal, "Libya: Al Qaeda-Linked Group Leader Found Dead," April 9, 2014, http://www.aafonline.co.za/news/libya-al-qaeda-linked-group-leader-found-dead; AND TRAC, "Islamic Youth Shura Council," accessed August 17, 2014, http://www.trackingterrorism.org/group/islamic-youth-shura-council; AND Aaron Y. Zelin, "The Islamic State's First Colony in Libya," October 10, 2014, The Washington Institute for Near East Policy, Policy Watch 2325, http://www.washingtoninstitute.org/policy-analysis/view/the-islamic-states-first-colony-in-libya

157 Aaron Y. Zelin, "The Islamic State's First Colony in Libya," The Washington Institute for Near East Policy, Policy Watch 2325, http://www.washingtoninstitute.org/policy-analysis/view/the-islamic-states-first-colony-in-libya

158 Homeland Security News Wire, "U.S. Concerns Grow as ISIS Establishes a Base of Operations in Libya," http://www.homelandsecuritynewswire.com/dr20141208-u-s-concerns-grow-as-isis-establishes-a-base-of-operations-in-libya

159 African Armed Forces Journal, "ISIS Divides Maghreb al-Qaeda (AQIM)," August 19, 2014, http://www.aafonline.co.za/news/isis-divides-maghreb-al-qaeda-aqim

160 Thomas Joscelyn, "Politico Jumps in the Benghazi Debate," December 30, 2013, The Weekly Standard, http://www.weeklystandard.com/print/blogs/politico-jumps-benghazi-debate_772398.html

161 Ludovico Carlino, "Profile of Libyan Terrorist Group Ansar al-Sharia – Ansar al-Shari'a: Transforming Libya into a Land of Jihad," Jan. 10, 2014, Terrorism Monitor, http://www.matthewaid.com/post/72882603307/profile-of-libyan-terrorist-group-ansar-al-sharia; AND Faisal Irshaid, "Profile: Libya's Ansar al-Sharia," updated June 13, 2014, BBC Monitoring, http://www.bbc.com/news/world-africa-27732589

162 African Armed Forces Journal, "ISIS Divides Maghreb al-Qaeda (AQIM)," August 19, 2014, http://www.aafonline.co.za/news/isis-divides-maghreb-al-qaeda-aqim; AND Aaron Y. Zelin, "Meeting Tunisia's Ansar al-Sharia," March 8, 2013, The Middle East Channel, carried on Jihadology Web site, http://jihadology.net/about/writings

163 Note 1: A puritanical form of Sunni Islam, the doctrine of Salafia Jihadia idealizes the first three generations of Muslims as the perfect Islamic community, and advocates reviving the venerated era of the Islamic forefathers via a succession of jihads with the sword against

infidel societies in order to restore the ummah's days of glory and its dominance over non-Muslims. The movement took hold in Morocco in the 1990s; since then, its doctrine, especially in the past several years, has swept into other areas of the Maghreb, such as in Algeria; and into the Sinai, Gaza, Saudi Arabia, and the Gulf area, as well as into other areas of the region. The doctrine is also taking hold abroad, especially in Europe. Note 2: Another trend sweeping the jihadist world is the Ansar movement: Instead of adopting unique names, groups refer to themselves as "Ansar," and in many cases "Ansar al-Sharia," thereby emphasizing the aim to establish an Islamic state. The newer wave of Ansar al-Sharia groups sprung up after April 2011. Global jihad ideologue, Shaykh Abu al-Mundhir al-Shinqiti, of Mauritanian origin, approvingly wrote in a June 2012 article titled, "We Are Ansar al-Sharia," that Muslims should establish da'wa and Ansar al-Sharia groups in their respective countries, and then join them all into a unified organization under the Ansar al-Sharia brand.

164 Aaron Y. Zelin, "Know Your Ansar al-Sharia," Sept. 21, 2012, The Washington Institute, http://www.washingtoninstitute.org/policy-analysis/view/know-your-ansar-al-sharia

165 Mawassi Lahcen, interview, "As al-Qaeda falls, Ansar al-Sharia rises," Oct. 5, 2012, Sabahi, http://sabahionline.com/en_GB/articles/hoa/articles/features/2012/10/05/feature-01

166 Abdullah Suleiman Ali, "Global Jihadists Recognize Islamic State," July 3, 2014, Al-Monitor, http://www.al-monitor.com/pulse/security/2014/07/syria-iraq-isis-islamic-caliphate-global-recognition.html#

167 Walid Ramzi, "West Africa: 'Caliphate' Claim Sparks New Jihadist Fighting," July 3, 2014, Magharebia, http://allafrica.com/stories/201407040589.html; AND Jemal Oumar, "Maghreb al-Qaeda Torn Apart by ISIS," August 15, 2014, http://magharebia.com/en_GB/articles/awi/reportage/2014/08/15/reportage-01

168 Candidates for the Council of Representatives parliamentary elections, June 25, 2014, were required to run as individuals; rather than on party lists, as was the case during the General National Congress parliamentary elections. The requirement was meant to mitigate further political polarization. International Foundation for Electoral Systems Election Guide, "Elections: Libya – Council of Representatives," accessed September 17, 2014, http://www.electionguide.org/countries/id/123; AND Security Council Report, "August 2014 Monthly Forecast: Libya," August 2014, http://www.securitycouncilreport.org/monthly-forecast/2014-08/libya_13.php?print=true

169 Libya's new unicameral parliament, the Majlis Al Nuwab or Council of Representatives, replaces the General National Congress (GNC) and serves as the new interim legislative authority during Libya's transitional period. The GNC was beleaguered by Islamist and allied militia strong-arm tactics. Replacing the GNC puts an end to the political dominance Muslim Brotherhood factions wielded in the legislature. International Foundation for Electoral

Systems, "Elections in Libya: June 25 Council of Representatives Elections Frequently Asked Questions," June 23, 2014, http://www.ifes.org/~/media/Files/Publications/White%20PaperReport/2014/2014_IFES _Libya%20Council%20of%20Representative%20Elections%20FAQs.pdf; AND Al Jazeera and Agencies, "Libya's Outgoing Parliament Elects PM," August 25, 2014, http://www.aljazeera.com/news/middleeast/2014/08/libya-outgoing-parliament-elects-pm-2014825134648296586.html

170 Violence in Tripoli caused the Council of Representatives to hold its first formal session on August 4, 2014 in the eastern city of Tobruk. The Tobruk meeting drew 158 of the 188 elected delegates. Parliament requires 200 seats, but 12 are unfilled because violence in those districts and boycotts prevented voting. The election outcome exacerbated tensions among militias affiliated with different political parties, and deepened the country's Islamist-nationalist cleavage. Current and former GNC lawmakers rejected the Tobruk parliamentary session as unconstitutional. The new Council of Representatives lacks a strong national army and police force to quell the fighting. David Kirkptrick and Suliman Ali Zway, "In Libya, Parliament Convenes Amid Battles," August 4, 2014, The New York Times, http://www.nytimes.com/2014/08/05/world/africa/libyas-new-parliament-meets-amid-militia-rivalries.html?_r=0; AND Patrick Markey and Aziz El Yaakoubi, "Libya's New Parliament Calls for Unity as Rival Militias Clash," August 4, 2014, Reuters, http://www.reuters.com/article/2014/08/05/us-libya-security-idUSKBN0G40YX20140805; AND Daily Nation, "Libya Parliament Meets in Eastern City of Tobruk, August 4, 2014

171 Areas of Tripoli took heavy artillery and rocket fire by the Islamist-leaning, Muslim Brotherhood-allied Misrata brigades battling to dislodge rival pro-secular, nationalist Zintan brigades. The Zintan brigades have a strong presence and control several key institutions and facilities in this capital port city; and they previously held some vital road intersections. Powerful and politically driven, these key militias receive government funding to serve in a quasi-official security capacity, but are locked in a geo-political struggle for dominance over the country. Turkish Weekly, "Libya Publishes Parliamentary Election Results," July 22, 2014, http://www.turkishweekly.net/print.asp?type=1&id=169449

172 Like other militias in Libya, the Zintan Brigades have been reluctant to cede power to the new authority because it has people from the old regime.

173 Homeland Security News Wire, "Islamists Seize Tripoli's Airport, Announce New Government," August 25, 2014, http://www.homelandsecuritynewswire.com/dr20140825-islamists-seize-tripoli-s-airport-announce-new-government; AND Chris Stephen and Anne Penketh, "Libyan Capital Under Islamist Control After Tripoli Airport Seized," August 24,

2014, The Guardian, http://www.theguardian.com/world/2014/aug/24/libya-capital-
under-islamist-control-tripoli-airport-seized-operation-dawn/print

174 Al Jazeera and Agencies, "Libya's Outgoing Parliament Elects PM," August 25, 2014,
http://www.aljazeera.com/news/middleeast/2014/08/libya-outgoing-parliament-elects-
pm-2014825134648296586.html

175 World Port Source, "Port of Tripoli: Review and History,"
http://www.worldportsource.com/ports/review/LBY_Port_of_Tripoli_661.php

176 Tom Stevenson, "Dozens Killed in Tripoli Suburb Under Siege," September 14, 2014, Al
Monitor, http://www.al-monitor.com/pulse/originals/2014/09/libya-tripoli-suburb-
siege.html#

177 Reuters, "East Libya Declares Self-Government," updated November 3, 2013, Al Jazeera,
http://www.aljazeera.com/news/africa/2013/11/east-libya-declares-self-government-
2013113195259621122.html

178 Since 2009, Libya has been on a worsening year-on-year trend across most country
indicators, according to the well-respected Fund For Peace not-for-profit research
organization's Failed State Index, now called Fragile State Index. In 2012, Libya was deemed
the "most worsened country" of 177 countries tracked; it ranked 50th on the country index,
with Somalia taking the #1 slot that indicated the most failed state status. From 2013 to
2014, Libya moved up the country index by +3.3 points toward state failure. Fund for Peace,
Country Date & Trends, "Libya in 2014," http://ffp.statesindex.org/2014-libya; AND
http://library.fundforpeace.org/libya

179 United States Energy Information Administration, "Libya: Overview," last updated October
10, 2013, http://www.eia.gov/countries/cab.cfm?fips=ly

180 Chris Stephen and Anne Penketh, "Libyan Capital Under Islamist Control After Tripoli
Airport Seized," August 24, 2014, The Guardian,
http://www.theguardian.com/world/2014/aug/24/libya-capital-under-islamist-control-
tripoli-airport-seized-operation-dawn/print

181 The Small Arms Survey is a project of the Graduate Institute of International and
Development Studies in Geneva. The publication is the principal international source of
information on small arms and armed violence, and a resource center for governments,
policymakers, researchers, and activists.

182 Small Arms Survey, "Armed Groups in Libya: Typology and Roles," June 2012,
http://www.smallarmssurvey.org/fileadmin/docs/H-Research_Notes/SAS-Research-Note-
18.pdf

183 George Washington University Homeland Security Policy Institute, "Somalia's Al-Shabaab: Down But Not Out," Issue Brief 22, August 27, 2013, Navanti Group, http://d383x9er2dcb4o.cloudfront.net/wp-content/uploads/2013/08/HSPI-Issue-Brief-22-Somalia-Al-Shabaab.pdf

184 Al-Shabaab is a hybrid organization because it is a locally focused and rooted Islamist insurgent group, as well as a transnational terrorist affiliate of Al Qa'ida.

185 Jonathan Masters, "Al-Shabab: Backgrounder," September 23, 2013, Council on Foreign Relations, http://www.cfr.org/somalia/al-shabab/p18650

186 The Al Qa'ida strategy of "glocalization" involves the lobbying of local and national militant groups in order to get them to reframe their anti-regime struggles in terms of the global jihad against the Zionist-Crusader alliance. Vahid Brown, "Self-Inflicted Wounds: Debates and Divisions within Al-Qa'ida and its Periphery," Chapter 4: Al-Qa'ida Central and Local Affiliates, pp 80-109, editors Assaf Moghadam and Brian Fishman, Dec. 16, 2010, https://www.ctc.usma.edu/posts/self-inflicted-wounds

187 There have been deep internal divisions and power struggles over embracing a nationalist versus a globalist agenda. There have also been ongoing clan-based rivalries within the group. Lauren Ploch Blanchard, "The September 2013 Terrorist Attack in Kenya: In Brief," November 14, 2013, Congressional Research Service, R43245, http://www.fas.org/sgp/crs/row/R43245.pdf; AND Graham Turbiville, Josh Meservey, and James Forest, "Countering the al-Shabaab Insurgency in Somalia: Lessons for U.S. Special Operations Forces," Joint Special Operations Report 14-1, February 2014, https://jsou.socom.mil/Documents/12-3_Jones_041112_FINAL.pdf

188 George Washington University Homeland Security Policy Institute, "Somalia's Al-Shabab: Down But Not Out," Issue Brief 22, August 27, 2013, Navanti Group, http://d383x9er2dcb4o.cloudfront.net/wp-content/uploads/2013/08/HSPI-Issue-Brief-22-Somalia-Al-Shabaab.pdf

189 On February 9, 2012, a video was released on jihadist Web sites; it featured an audio recording by Al-Shabaab co-founder, Ahmed Abdi Aw-Mohamed aka Godane, addressing AQ leader Ayman al-Zawahiri and pledging allegiance to him, as well as an announcement from al-Zawahiri stating that Al-Shabaab joined Qa'idat al-Jihad aka AQ. Aw-Mohamed consolidated control over Al-Shabaab by eliminating some rivals and by purging other rivals from the group, and he exercised command responsibility for Al-Shabaab's operations across Somalia until he was killed in a U.S. targeted airstrike on September 1, 2014 at a training camp south of Mogadishu. Nelly Lahoud, "The Merger of Al-Shabab and Qa'idat Al-Jihad," February 16, 2012, CTC Sentinel, http://www.ctc.usma.edu/posts/the-merger-of-al-shabab-and-qaidat-al-jihad; AND UNSC Sanctions List, "List of Individuals and Entities Subject to the

Measures Imposed by Paragraphs 1, 3 and 7 of Security Council Resolution 1844 (2008),"
March 11, 2014, http://www.un.org/sc/committees/751/pdf/1844_cons_list.pdf; AND Bill
Roggio, "US Confirms Shabaab Emir Godane Killed in Airstrike," September 5, 2014, The
Long War Journal,
http://www.longwarjournal.org/archives/2014/09/us_confirms_shabaab-print.php.

190 Ahmad Umar is believed to be from Ahmed Abdi Aw-Mohamed's hardline inner circle and
served as his close adviser. His appointment is believed to be causing factional rivalries
within the group. United Nations Security Council, "Report of the Monitoring Group on
Somalia and Eritrea Pursuant to Security Council Resolution 2111 (2013): Somalia," general
distribution October 13, 2014, Report No. S/2014/726,
http://www.un.org/ga/search/view_doc.asp?symbol=S/2014/726

191 Less than a week after Al-Shabaab co-founder Ahmed Abdi Aw-Mohamed aka Godane was
killed in an airstrike on September 1, 2014, the terrorist group announced that Sheikh
Ahmad Umar aka Abu Ubaidah was the its new emir. Thomas Joscelyn, "Shabaab Names New
Emir, Reaffirms Allegiance to Al Qaeda," September 6, 2014, The Long War Journal,
http://www.longwarjournal.org/archives/2014/09/shabaab_names_new_em-print.php

192 Original military commander, Adan Ayro, modeled Al-Shabaab's principles after the Taliban
after training in Afghanistan. In 2013, there were frequent reports that this terrorist group
carried out amputation of limbs for minor thievery offenses, stoning for suspected adultery,
killings of converts to religions other than Islam, and forced conscription of child soldiers.
U.S. Department of State Country Reports on Terrorism 2013, April 2014,
http://www.state.gov/documents/organization/225886.pdf

193 Associate Press, "Senior Emirati Official Warns of Possibility of Islamic State and Al-Shabab
Collaboration, October 29, 2014, Fox News,
http://www.foxnews.com/world/2014/10/29/senior-emirati-official-warns-possibility-
islamic-state-and-al-shabab

194 Associated Press, "UAE Official Warns of Potential for Islamic State, Al-Shabab Link," October
29, 2014, Al Arabiya News, http://english.alarabiya.net/en/News/2014/10/29/UAE-
official-warns-of-potential-for-ISIS-Shabab-link.html

195 Abdi Moalim, "New Al-Shabaab Leader's Silence Sparks Speculation," October 31, 2014,
Sabahi,
http://sabahionline.com/en_GB/articles/hoa/articles/features/2014/10/31/feature-01

196 United Nations Security Council, "Report of the Monitoring Group on Somalia and Eritrea
Pursuant to Security Council Resolution 2111 (2013): Somalia," general distribution October

13, 2014, Report No. S/2014/726,
http://www.un.org/ga/search/view_doc.asp?symbol=S/2014/726

197 Despite the targeted airstrikes, Al-Shabaab's senior leadership is still intact and can move freely throughout Somalia. Al-Shabaab has used foreign counter-terrorism operations to suit its propaganda purposes. For instance, the group released in August 2014 a documentary-style video reconstructing the abortive January 11, 2013 France-United States military raid on Bulo Marer. United Nations Security Council, "Report of the Monitoring Group on Somalia and Eritrea Pursuant to Security Council Resolution 2111 (2013): Somalia," general distribution October 13, 2014, Report No. S/2014/726, http://www.un.org/ga/search/view_doc.asp?symbol=S/2014/726

198 United Nations Security Council, "Report of the Monitoring Group on Somalia and Eritrea Pursuant to Security Council Res 2060 (2012) - Somalia, July 12 2013," Report S/2013/413, http://reliefweb.int/report/somalia/report-monitoring-group-somalia-and-eritrea-pursuant-security-council-resolution-2060; AND United States Department of State Country Reports on Terrorism 2013, April 2014, http://www.state.gov/documents/organization/225886.pdf; AND International Crisis Group, "Somalia: Al-Shabaab – It will be a Long War," June 26, 2014, Africa Policy Briefing No. 99, http://www.crisisgroup.org/~/media/Files/africa/horn-of-africa/somalia/b099-somalia-al-shabaab-it-will-be-a-long-war.pdf

199 United Nations Security Council, "Report of the Monitoring Group on Somalia and Eritrea Pursuant to Security Council Resolution 2111 (2013): Somalia," general distribution October 13, 2014, Report No. S/2014/726, http://www.un.org/ga/search/view_doc.asp?symbol=S/2014/726

200 Somalia's eastern and northern coastlines are more than 2,000 miles long.

201 AMISOM and Somali National Army forces renewed joint initiative, Operation Indian Ocean, began on September 1, 2014. Since the new operation, the joint forces have liberated six strategic towns from Al-Shabaab. African Union Mission in Somalia, "Somalia National Army and AMISOM Forces Liberate Adale Town in Middle Shebelle Region," October 3, 2014, http://amisom-au.org/2014/10/somalia-national-army-and-amisom-forces-liberate-adale-town-in-middle-shebelle-region

202 On October 5, 2014, it was reported that the African Union and Somali troops took control of the important southern port town of Barawe from Al-Shabaab after a series of gun and bombing attacks in Mogadishu. The strategic port had been under Al-Shabaab's control since 2006, and activities there have included the terrorist group's multi-million dollar illicit charcoal trade and the importation of supplies for the Islamist militants. This area also has been a safe haven and a training ground for bombers. Feisal Omar, "African Union and

Somali Forces Claim Shabaab Stronghold of Barawe," October 5, 2014, Reuters, http://uk.reuters.com/article/2014/10/05/uk-somalia-security-shabaab-idUKKCN0HU0C720141005

203 The Somali National Army and AMISOM forces liberated Cadale, aka Adale, as part of Operation Indian Ocean. African Union Mission in Somalia, "Somalia National Army and AMISOM Forces Liberate Adale Town in Middle Shebelle Region," October 3, 2014, http://amisom-au.org/2014/10/somalia-national-army-and-amisom-forces-liberate-adale-town-in-middle-shebelle-region

204 Reporting by AMISOM Joint Operation Information-Sharing Forum, sections 18-20 and footnotes 22-23. United Nations Security Council, "Report of the Monitoring Group on Somalia and Eritrea Pursuant to Security Council Resolution 2111 (2013): Somalia," general distribution October 13, 2014, Report No. S/2014/726, http://www.un.org/ga/search/view_doc.asp?symbol=S/2014/726

205 African Armed Forces journal, "Government Forces, Al Shabaab in Fierce Fight Over Strategic Island," November 10, 2014, http://www.aafonline.co.za/news/government-forces-al-shabaab-fierce-fight-over-strategic-island

206 Puntland is a criminalized, semi-autonomous, de facto state that broke away from Somalia in 1998 and has not been recognized by the international community.

207 Per a briefing by the Somalia-Eritrea Monitoring Groups with Puntland diplomats, and per confidential United Nations reports. United Nations Security Council, "Report of the Monitoring Group on Somalia and Eritrea Pursuant to Security Council Resolution 2111 (2013): Somalia," general distribution October 13, 2014, Report No. S/2014/726, http://www.un.org/ga/search/view_doc.asp?symbol=S/2014/726

208 Somali Water and Land Information Management, "Monitoring of the Golis Mountain Forest in Somalia," December 2010, Technical Rep. No. L-18, http://sddr.faoswalim.org/sddr/Documents_Repository/land_reports/L-18%20Monitoring%20of%20Golis%20Forest%20in%20Somalia_The%20Report.pdf

209 United States. Department of State Country Reports on Terrorism 2013, April 2014, http://www.state.gov/documents/organization/225886.pdf

210 Under militia leader Yassin Khalid Osman, the Galgala Militia has been fighting the Christian government in this autonomous region. Assia Shidane, "What is the Galgala Conflict?" April 13, 2012, Somali Report, http://www.somaliareport.com/index.php/post/3240

211 BBC reported on October 1, 2014 that after a heavy battle ensued for the Galgala Mountains, Al-Shabaab and Puntland information minister, Abdiweli Hirsi Abdille, claimed to have won

the contest. BBC News, "Somalia Battles Al-Shabab for Galgala Mountains," October 1, 2014, http://www.bbc.com/news/world-africa-29444355

212 Somaliland authorities are investigating renewed Al-Shabaab infiltration into Sool after arresting the terrorist group's key Amniyat operative Ahmed Mohamud aka Arabey sometime around 2014. Mohamud was alleged to be recruiting on behalf of Al-Shabaab in Somaliland. United Nations Security Council, "Report of the Monitoring Group on Somalia and Eritrea Pursuant to Security Council Resolution 2111 (2013): Somalia," general distribution October 13, 2014, Report No. S/2014/726, http://www.un.org/ga/search/view_doc.asp?symbol=S/2014/726

213 Ryan Mauro, "Al-Qaeda Seizes Town in Teetering Yemen," April 4, 2011, Front Page Magazine, http://www.frontpagemag.com/2011/ryan-mauro/al-qaeda-seizes-town-in-teetering-yemen; AND Oren Adaki, "AQAP Capitalizes on the Chaos in Yemen," October 10, 2014, http://defenddemocracy.org/media-hit/oren-adaki-aqap-capitalizes-on-the-chaos-in-yemen

214 Al-Shabaab is able to coordinate and conduct attacks throughout the Horn of Africa, and retains the operational capacity to target Westerners in Djibouti, Kenya, and other countries. African Armed Forces journal, "Al Shabab Changes Tactics in Response to Increased Pressure," October 14, 2014, http://www.aafonline.co.za/news/al-shabaab-changes-tactics-response-increased-pressure; AND, Global Post, "African Militants Learn from Al Qaeda in Yemen," September 10, 2012, http://www.globalpost.com/dispatch/news/regions/africa/120907/al-qaeda-al-shabaab-somalia; AND George Washington University Homeland Security Policy Institute, "Somalia's Al-Shabab: Down But Not Out," Issue Brief 22, August 27, 2013, Navanti Group, http://d383x9er2dcb4o.cloudfront.net/wp-content/uploads/2013/08/HSPI-Issue-Brief-22-Somalia-Al-Shabaab.pdf

215 International Crisis Group, "Somalia: Al-Shabaab – It will be a Long War," June 26, 2014, Africa Policy Briefing No. 99, http://www.crisisgroup.org/~/media/Files/africa/horn-of-africa/somalia/b099-somalia-al-shabaab-it-will-be-a-long-war.pdf

216 Al-Shabaab has two local radio stations, Al-Andus and Alfurqaan, with complementing Web sites; several other Web sites: Amiirnuur, Somalimidnimo, and Somalimemo; the Shahada News Agency, a Twitter account, and multimedia content. UNSC - Report of the Monitoring Group on Somalia and Eritrea Pursuant to Security Council Res 2060 (2012) - Somalia, July 12 2013, Report S/2013/413, http://reliefweb.int/report/somalia/report-monitoring-group-somalia-and-eritrea-pursuant-security-council-resolution-2060

217 George Washington University Homeland Security Policy Institute, "Somalia's Al-Shabab: Down But Not Out," Issue Brief 22, August 27, 2013, Navanti Group,

http://d383x9er2dcb4o.cloudfront.net/wp-content/uploads/2013/08/HSPI-Issue-Brief-22-
Somalia-Al-Shabaab.pdf; AND Christopher Anzalone, "The Life and Death of Al-Shabab
Leader Ahmed Godane," September 2014, Counter-terrorism Sentinel, Vol. 7, Issue 9,
https://www.ctc.usma.edu/posts/the-life-and-death-of-al-shabab-leader-ahmed-godane

218 Al-Shabaab 's diverse fiscal base is a result of the following KEY sources of support: (1)
Illegal charcoal trade – the primary source of finance, according to a United Nations report
cited in the African Armed Forces journal, which informed on June 26, 2014 that the terrorist
group brings in between $38 million and $68 million annually from charcoal sales and
taxation; (2) Taxation – willing support, including via zakat or mandatory Islamic charity;
extortion of local businesses and of international relief organizations in areas under the
terrorist group's control; and partnership of businesses, international humanitarian
agencies and local non-governmental organizations; (2) External support – (a) global
jihadists mainly concentrated in the Arabian Peninsula; (b) remittances from the Somali
diaspora; (c) state sponsorship from Eritrea, although Eritrea's support has been on the
decline. Other state and non-state sponsors include Djibouti, Iran, Syria, Libya, Egypt, Saudi
Arabia, Al Qa'ida and Hizb'allah, which have provided Al-Shabaab with weapons, missiles,
and training; (3) Weapons – (a) Al-Shabaab has a monopoly over the trafficking of illegal
weapons in Kenya; (b) Mohamed Sa'id aka Atom is one of the principal suppliers of arms and
ammunition for Al-Shabaab operations in the Puntland region. SOURCES: [1] African Armed
Forces journal, "UN: Illegal Wildlife and Charcoal Trade Funding Global Terror Groups," June
26, 2014, http://www.aafonline.co.za/news/un-illegal-wildlife-and-charcoal-trade-funding-
global-terror-groups; [2] Ken Menkhaus, "Al-Shabab's Capabilities Post-Westgate," February
2014, CTC Sentinel, https://www.ctc.usma.edu/wp-content/uploads/2014/02/CTCSentinel-
Vol7Iss2.pdf; AND U.S. Department of the Treasury Press Center, "Treasury Targets Regional
Actors Fueling Violence and Instability in Somalia," July 5, 2012,
http://www.treasury.gov/press-center/press-releases/Pages/tg1630.aspx; AND Graham
Turbiville, Josh Meservey, and James Forest, "Countering the al-Shabaab Insurgency in
Somalia: Lessons for U.S. Special Operations Forces," Joint Special Operations Report 14-1,
February 2014, https://jsou.socom.mil/Documents/12-3_Jones_041112_FINAL.pdf; [3]
William Allen, "Al-Shabaab and the Exploitation of the Subject Network Model," May 9, 2014,
Small Wars Journal, http://smallwarsjournal.com/print/15373; AND UNSC Sanctions List,
"List of Individuals and Entities Subject to the Measures Imposed by Paragraphs 1, 3 and 7 of
Security Council Resolution 1844 (2008)," March 11, 2014,
http://www.un.org/sc/committees/751/pdf/1844_cons_list.pdf

219 Al-Shabaab has tried to win support of local communities and leaders by providing services
that the Somali government has failed to provide, including mobile Sharia courts to settle
disputes, building infrastructure, repairing roads, organizing markets, and passing out food
and money to the poor; it uses this engagement for propaganda purposes. However, during

the 2010-2012 famine in Somalia, Al-Shabaab blocked international food aid distribution, which resulted in the group losing some local support.

220 Al-Shabaab inspires and incites potential recruits by teaching them that ethnic Somalis have been reduced to mere economic Muslim subjects of the West; that Islam is under attack by the West and they resultantly have a personal responsibility to wage jihad; and Somalis have historically been resistance fighters against Western colonialists. William Allen, "Al-Shabaab and the Exploitation of the Subject Network Model," May 9, 2014, Small Wars Journal, http://smallwarsjournal.com/print/15373

221 Somali expatriate communities, particularly in Djibouti and Ethiopia, according to the Somalia-Eritrea Monitoring Group, serve as Al-Shabaab Amniyat (the terrorist group's secret service arm)-like, operatives, including diplomats, journalists, and community activists therein. There are also affiliates, such as Al-Hijra, formerly the once ostensibly benign Muslim Youth Center (MYC), which is serving as Al-Shabaab 's East Africa affiliate. Al Hijra consists of hundreds of recruits from Kenya and from neighboring countries who train under Al-Shabaab, but whose grievances and targets are in East Africa. This wing of Al-Shabaab carried out the deadly July 2010 bombings in Kampala, Uganda. Al Hijra controls the Eastleigh neighborhood of Nairobi, Kenya, from where the September 2013 Westgate shopping mall attack was executed by Al-Shabaab, in coordination with Al-Hijra. There is also an informal Al-Shabaab affiliate based in Nairobi called Masjid-ul-Axmari. This group is led by Imam Hasan Mahat Omar aka Sheikh Hassan Hussein. The United Nations informed that Omar recruits new members and solicits funds for Al-Shabaab, including online at the Al-Shabaab affiliated Web site Alqimmah.net. Kenya is experiencing a growing number of Al-Shabaab recruits, including in Mombasa; and there is a growing number of Al-Shabaab recruits in the United Republic of Tanzania. The monitoring group expressed its extreme concern at the use of UN camps for terrorist safe havens and staging groups for Al-Shabaab operations. Al-Shabaab is also involved in a criminal network of pirate leaders and illegal fishers engaged in trafficking in the Gulf of Aden. Ken Menkhaus, "Al-Shabab's Capabilities Post-Westgate," February 2014, CTC Sentinel, https://www.ctc.usma.edu/wp-content/uploads/2014/02/CTCSentinel-Vol7Iss2.pdf; AND UNSC Sanctions List, "List of Individuals and Entities Subject to the Measures Imposed by Paragraphs 1, 3 and 7 of Security Council Resolution 1844 (2008)," March 11, 2014, http://www.un.org/sc/committees/751/pdf/1844_cons_list.pdf; AND United Nations Security Council, "Report of the Monitoring Group on Somalia and Eritrea Pursuant to Security Council Resolution 2111 (2013): Somalia," general distribution October 13, 2014, Report No. S/2014/726, http://www.un.org/ga/search/view_doc.asp?symbol=S/2014/726

222 Paul D. Williams, "Is al-Shabaab Resurgent or Weakening? A Tale of Two Narratives," June 10, 2014, http://theglobalobservatory.org/analysis/760-is-al-shabaab-resurgent-or-weakening-a-tale-of-two-narratives.html

223 Before emir Ahmed Abdi Aw-Mohamed met his demise in September 2014, this unchallenged leader systematically purged Al-Shabaab of dissenters in order to consolidate his authority. The purge apparently gave space for the more militant elements to dominate the group, a factor likely strengthened by the militarizing trend of Islamist groups in the region.

224 For example: the September 2013 Westgate mall attack in Nairobi, Kenya. The Somalia-Eritrea Monitoring Group described Al-Shabaab as "operationally audacious" and placing emphasis on exporting its violence beyond Somalia; the monitoring group informed that despite the terrorist group's inability to recover its military strength and posture during the height of its might from 2009-2010, it still generates fatal attacks in southern and central Somalia, and still inspires and coordinates attacks abroad. Section 24, United Nations Security Council, "Report of the Monitoring Group on Somalia and Eritrea Pursuant to Security Council Resolution 2111 (2013): Somalia," general distribution October 13, 2014, Report No. S/2014/726, http://www.un.org/ga/search/view_doc.asp?symbol=S/2014/726

225 For instance, to compensate for its reduced force strength, Al-Shabaab typically avoids direct military engagements with AMISOM and Somali National Army forces; it now uses reliable and low-risk magnetic improvised explosive devices, and employs targeted killings in order to elevate an atmosphere of fear in Mogadishu. Also, Al-Shabaab has graduated from randomly targeting rank and file Somali National Armed Forces (SNAF) to high profile targets against senior government and security officials; it has been conducting high-profile attacks against government structures, such as the Presidential Palace and the Somali Federal Parliament; and it has infiltrated the SNAF and the Federal Government of Somalia at the highest and most sensitive levels in order to spread fear, to intimidate, and to create a destabilizing atmosphere. "... You will have nowhere to run," Al-Shabaab reportedly warned Members of Parliament, adding, "Allah says fight the non-believers and target their leaders." United Nations Security Council, "Report of the Monitoring Group on Somalia and Eritrea Pursuant to Security Council Resolution 2111 (2013): Somalia," general distribution October 13, 2014, Report No. S/2014/726, http://www.un.org/ga/search/view_doc.asp?symbol=S/2014/726

226 The Somalia-Eritrea Monitoring Group reports that in addition to Al-Shabaab facing a surge from AMISOM, and engagements by armed forces in Somalia, the group also must contend with periodic counter-terrorism operations from Ethiopia, Kenya, and the United States. United Nations Security Council, "Report of the Monitoring Group on Somalia and Eritrea Pursuant to Security Council Resolution 2111 (2013): Somalia," general distribution October

13, 2014, Report No. S/2014/726,
http://www.un.org/ga/search/view_doc.asp?symbol=S/2014/726

227 According to Forbes Israel IS is the wealthiest terrorist organization in the world, with a net worth of $2 billion. Among the groups researched in this article, the Taliban, AQ and affiliates, Al-Shabaab, and Boko Haram are included in its list of the world's top 10 richest terrorist organizations. Tova Dorin, "Hamas Second-Richest Terror Group Worldwide," November 11, 2014, Israel National News,
http://www.israelnationalnews.com/News/News.aspx/187337#.VGOKsSjzj6k

228 Many states in these regions have enormously high percentages of youth under the age of 25 years, and many of these youth are unemployed.

229 An example of how Islamist unions and Muslim youth centers can evolve and become more militant: The Islamic Court Union was the mother organization to Al-Shabaab, its military wing that in September 2007 split from the union. Al-Shabaab went on to absorb several supposedly "moderate" Muslim groups, including the Muslim Youth Center (MYC), which rebranded as Al Hirja in 2012. In January 2012, MYC merged with the Tanzanian Ansaar Muslim Youth Center; and the day after Al Qa'ida and Al-Shabaab announced their merger in February 2012, the MYC announced that it became "part of al Qaeda East Africa." Al-Shabaab also has ties with the Community of Muslim Organizations in Tanzania, with the terrorist group maintaining, at the very least, technical and some material support to this organization. Thomas Joscelyn and Bill Roggio, " 'We in MYC are now part of al Qaeda East Africa,' " Feb. 10, 2012, The Long War Journal,
http://www.longwarjournal.org/archives/2012/02/we_in_myc_are_now_pa.php#; AND Dominic Wabala, "Kenya: Majengo Youth 'Recruiting Terrorists,'" July 19, 2012, All Africa, http://allafrica.com/stories/201207200109.ht; AND African Armed Forces Journal, Issue 1, "Al-Hijra - The Rise of the Islamic Threat in Kenya," Nov. 18, 2013,
http://www.aafonline.co.za/insights/al-hijra---rise-islamic-threat-kenya; AND Ken Menkhaus, "Al-Shabab's Capabilities Post-Westgate," February 2014, CTC Sentinel, https://www.ctc.usma.edu/wp-content/uploads/2014/02/CTCSentinel-Vol7Iss2.pdf; AND IHS Jane's Intelligence Weekly, "Large-scale Attacks by Domestic Militant Groups Unlikely but Sectarian Violence Increases in Tanzania, February 27, 2014,
http://www.janes.com/article/34706/large-scale-attacks-by-domestic-militant-groups-unlikely-but-sectarian-violence-increases-in-tanzania

230 This author has conducted extensive research on Islam and nuclear weapons and has plans to publish this work in an upcoming book.

231 The term implies Shi'ites are rejectionists. The Muslim ummah split into Sunnis and Shi'a due to a succession controversy over who would lead them. The majority of Muslims –

Sunnis – chose Muhammad's close companion and father-in-law, Abu Bakr, as their first caliph or political-social leader. The minority Muslims – Shi'ites – believed succession had to go through Muhammad's bloodline; they chose his cousin and son-in-law, 'Ali ibn Abu Talib, as their first imam or spiritual leader, which the Sunnis finally chose as their fourth caliph. Twelver Shi'ites are the majority Shi'a sect. They recognize 12 supreme authorities descended from Muhammad: 'Ali ibn Abu Talib, his two sons Hassan and Husayn, and a succession of nine of Husayn's descendants. The Twelvers consider these imams infallible. The last and 12th imam, Muhammad, inherited the title "al-mahdi" or messiah, and they believe he went into occultation, and will emerge during the Islamic Judgment Day to lead Muslims in a supreme and climatic jihad to wipe out all perceived forces of evil and to usher in a New World Islamic Order. Hussein Abdulwaheed Amin, "The origins of the Sunni/Shia split in Islam," 2001, http://cdn.preterhuman.net/texts/religion.occult.new_age/Islam/The%20Origins%20of%20the%20Sunni-Shia%20split%20in%20Islam.pdf; AND Butler, "The origins of the Sunni-Shi'ite split," 2007, http://www.flowofhistory.com/%5Bmenupathalias%5D/fc46a; AND Christopher M. Blanchard, "Islam: Sunnis and Shiites," January 28, 2009, Congressional Research Service Rep. No. RS21745, http://www.fas.org/irp/crs/RS21745.pdf; AND British Broadcasting Corporation, "Sunni and Shi'a," 2009, http://www.bbc.co.uk/religion/religions/islam/subdivisions/sunnishia_1.shtml; AND Imad Salamey and Zanoubia Othman, "Shia revival and Welayat Al-Faqih in the making of Iranian foreign policy," 2011, Politics, Religion & Ideology, 12(2), 197-212. doi: 10.1080/21567689.2011.591983

232 Other IS targets mentioned in the caliphate announcement include apostates and the U.S.-backed Awakening Councils.

233 This author has conducted extensive research on Islam and nuclear weapons and has plans to publish this work in a book.

234 This author warned the U.S. Congress and in the White House about this phenomenon in 2009 in an analysis entitled: "Revolutionary Islam and the Arab-Israeli Conflict," which focused on how a "two state solution" birthing a hostile Arab state in the Jewish ancestral homeland would severely weaken Israel, and enable Muslim terrorist groups to forge a caliphate spanning Asia and Africa. One of the maps this author landscaped therein looks very much like the IS map today.

235 Deputy Dean of the International Counter-Terrorism Institute, Dr. (Col.) Eitan Azani, Terrorism Fundraising lectures, 2012.

236 Sending Saudi funding and exporting the Wahhabi ideology and its militants to theaters of global jihad slowed down somewhat after the September 11, 2001 attacks on the United

States because the outrage brought the kingdom under greater scrutiny. However, the Saudi policy remains in force; particularly since 2003, when AQ attacked Riyadh and made it clear that the House of Saud was the near enemy, which prompted the royal family to implement domestic only counter-terrorism operations, and to continue its support of terrorism abroad.

237 See for instance, "Explain, Mr President: Obama Pulls References to Islam from Terror Training Manuals, But Orders Killing of Awlaki," by Pamela Geller, Atlas Shrugs, October 23, 2011, http://pamelageller.com/2011/10/explain-mr-president-obama-pulls-references-to-islam-from-terror-training-materials-but-orders-killi.html; AND "Emerson, IPT Expose Brennan Letter: FBI Training 'Substandard and Offensive' to Muslims, by Awr Hawkins, February 8, 2013, http://www.breitbart.com/big-government/2013/02/08/nov-3-2011-letter-from-john-brennan-capitulating-to-muslim-complaints-against-fbi

238 See for instance, "Exclusive: Senior U.S. General Orders Top-to-Bottom Review of Military's Islam Training," by Spencer Ackerman, April 24, 2012, Danger Room, http://www.wired.com/2012/04/military-islam-training

239 See for instance, "Georgetown University Panel Shows How Islamic State's Caliphate Has Justification in Islamic History and Appeal for Modern Muslims," by Andrew Harrod, November 11, 2014, http://www.jihadwatch.org/2014/11/georgetown-university-panel-shows-how-islamic-states-caliphate-has-justification-in-islamic-history-and-appeal-for-modern-muslims

240 June 1, 2009 – drive-by shootings targeting soldiers outside military recruiting station: 1 soldier killed, 1 wounded by lone gunman. He was arrested with semi-automatic rifle, .22-caliber rifle, and handgun. "Gunman Kills Soldier Outside Recruiting Station," by Steve Barnes and James Dao, The New York Times, June 1, 2009, http://www.nytimes.com/2009/06/02/us/02recruit.html?_r=0

241 November 5, 2009 – shootings by U.S. Army major/psychiatrist in combat uniform targeting personnel at Fort Hood military base: 13 killed, 32 wounded by perpetrator. Perpetrator shot, paralyzed; received salary until found guilty, sentenced to death August 28, 2013. His victims to date are denied combat-related pay, benefits. Pentagon labeled rapid fire shooting spree workplace violence. Note: April 2, 2014 – shootings targeting personnel at same base: 3 killed, 16 wounded by perpetrator, who died of self-inflicted gunshot wound. Perpetrator was Iraq war veteran who served in non-combat position and was under psychiatric treatment. He purchased a .45 pistol for shooting rampage at same gun shop perpetrator of 2009 Fort Hood shooting purchased his. "Victims Want 2009 Fort Hood Shooting Deemed Terror Act," by Associate Press, October 19, 2012, http://www.foxnews.com/us/2012/10/19/victims-want-200-fort-hood-shooting-deemed-

terror-act;" AND "Accused Fort Hood Shooter Paid $278,000 While Awaiting Trial," by Scott Friedman, May 22, 2013, http://www.nbcdfw.com/investigations/Accused-Fort-Hood-Shooter-Paid-278000-While-Awaiting-Trial-208230691.html; AND "But Why? The Search for a Motive in the Fort Hood Mass Shooting,
Reuters, April 4, 2014, http://www.newsweek.com/why-search-motive-fort-hood-mass-shooting-244245

242 March 11, 15, and 19, 2012 – shootings from motorcyclist targeting soldiers; and a rabbi, and Jewish children at a Jewish school: 7 killed, 5 injured, 2 seriously, by perpetrator. Perpetrator filmed his three separate attacks and was killed during shootout with paramilitary police. "Mohammed Merah, Taulouse Killing Spree Suspect, Killed by Police in Shootout," by Edward Cody, The Washington Post, March 22, 2012, http://www.washingtonpost.com/world/europe/mohammed-merah-shooting-suspect-wants-to-die-fighting-official-says/2012/03/22/gIQAJkYCTS_story.html

243 April 15, 2013 – two perpetrators detonate twin bombs at Boston Marathon finish line during race: 3 killed, 264 wounded. Perpetrators also accused of killing MIT police officer before attempting to flee. Perpetrators were brothers: older brother killed by police during 4-day manhunt, he had Internet ties with 2 jihadists who were killed in counterterrorism raids weeks before Boston bombing; younger brother awaiting trial, faces 30 charges, 17 carrying possible death penalty. Sources: "Boston Bombing Trial May Hold Answer to Radical Roots," by Jeff Swicord, January 10, 2015, http://www.voanews.com/content/boston-bombing-trial-may-hold-answer-to-radical-roots/2593181.html ; AND "More Potential Jurors Summoned for Tsarnaev Trial," by Milton J. Valencia, January 6, 2015, Boston Globe, http://www.bostonglobe.com/metro/2015/01/06/dzhokhar-tsarnaev-jury-selection-continues-tuesday-boston-marathon-bombing-case/Mg6NG0N6QqCYsATAx2Pell/story.html; AND The National Counterterrorism Center 2014 Calendar, http://www.nctc.gov/site/pdfs/ct_calendar_2014.pdf

244 May 22, 2013 – two perpetrators execute car/knife/meat cleaver attack targeting soldier near Royal Artillery Barracks adjacent to Woolwich Common, home of Royal Artillery: 1 soldier targeted, killed by 2 perpetrators. Dozens of witnesses watch perpetrators ambush soldier in daylight by driving up on sidewalk and ramming him into a sign with their car, alighting from car, then stabbing, hacking, and trying to behead soldier with machete-style knives and meat cleavers. Perpetrators demand that witnesses film them while waiting 20 minutes for police, then charged at responding officers with old hand gun, knives, meat cleavers. Two perpetrators shot by female markswoman of Scotland Yard's elite CO19 unit, arrested, hospitalized with serious injuries. British Prime Minister said attack was "betrayal of Islam." " 'You and Your Children will be Next': Islamic Fanatics Wielding Meat Cleavers

Butcher and Try to Behead a British Soldier, Taking Their War on the West to a New Level of Horror," by Arthur Martin, Sam Greenhill, Chris Greenwood, and Rob Cooper, Daily Mail, updated May 23, 2013, http://www.dailymail.co.uk/news/article-2329089/Woolwich-attack-Two-men-hack-soldier-wearing-Help-Heroes-T-shirt-death-machetes-suspected-terror-attack.html

245 On or around April 27 and on June 1, 2014 in Washington state, and on June 25, 2014 in New Jersey – civilian-targeted shootings: 4 killed by perpetrator. Shooting spree spanning both states: Circa April 27, first victim gunned down near his Skyway, Washington home. On June 1, perpetrator lured a homosexual couple to a Seattle, Washington nightclub, left with them in one of the victims' car, and then shot them. June 25, in West Orange, New Jersey, perpetrator, a fugitive at the time, killed a college student sitting at a traffic light, shooting him 8 times; two others arrested in this case. The main perpetrator is alleged to have ties to a disrupted Islamic terrorist cell, and to an Islamic terrorist training camp in Bly, Oregon. "Seattle Man Says He Killed 4 in Wash., N.J. to Gain Revenge Against U.S.," by James Queally, August 20, 2014, http://touch.latimes.com/#section/-1/article/p2p-81137814; AND Superior Court of Washington for King County, The State of Washington v. Ali Muhammad Brown, No. 14-1-03028-9-SEA, http://touch.latimes.com/#section/-1/article/p2p-81137814; AND "Murder Suspect on Personal Jihad May Have Been Groomed in Seattle Barber Shop," by Pamela Browne, November 4, 2014, Fox News, http://www.foxnews.com/us/2014/11/04/murder-suspect-on-personal-jihad-may-have-been-groomed-in-seattle-barber-shop

246 May 24, 2014 – shootings targeting civilians in Jewish museum; 4 killed by perpetrator: Shooter with Kalashnikov rifle drove up to the museum, went inside and opened fire, then fled the scene in his vehicle. He killed 2 museum workers (one had been in critical condition), and a couple from Israel. The perpetrator was arrested several days after the terrorist attack, and was found with a white sheet emblazoned with the name of ISIS. He was identified as one of the captors and torturers of James Foley and Steve Sotloff by a French journalist who was released after a nearly a year in IS captivity. The journalist said the perpetrator was one of several French citizens in charge of the prison where he was held captive. "The torture lasted the night, up until the dawn prayer," the journalist informed. The perpetrator fought for IS in 2013, only three weeks after he was released from prison for serving time for armed robbery. The Czech president blamed the attack on Islamic ideology, and added that "one of the sacred texts of Islam calls for killing Jews." "Two Israelis Among Three Killed in Brussels Museum Attack," ny Anshel Pfeffer, Barak Ravid, Haaretz, May 25, 2014, http://www.haaretz.com/jewish-world/jewish-world-news/1.592541; AND "Zeman: Islam is to Blame for Attack on Jewish Museum in Brussels," by Czech News Agency, May 27, 2014, http://www.praguepost.com/eu-news/39288-zeman-islam-is-to-blame-for-attack-on-jewish-museum-in-brussels; AND "ISIS Terrorist Identified as Murderer in Brussels

Jewish Museum Attack," by Tzvi Ben-Gedalyahu, updated September 7, 2014, The Jewish Press, http://www.jewishpress.com/news/breaking-news/isis-terrorist-identified-as-murderer-in-brussels-jewish-museum-attack/2014/09/06

247 September 23, 2014 – stabbings targeting counter-terrorism police officers; 2 wounded by perpetrator: Perpetrator attacked the officers outside Endeavour Hills police station in Melbourne after police arranged to meet with him to discuss his recently canceled Australian passport. The perpetrator stabbed the Victoria Police officer in the arm and the Australian Federal Police officer in the chest and face. He was on top of the AFP officer when the Victoria Police officer shot and killed him. Earlier, the perpetrator was alleged to have made threats against Prime Minister Tony Abbott, and to have displayed IS flags. "Abdul Numan Haider was 'Stabbing a Police Officer' When He Was Shot," by Australian Associated Press, October 2, 2014, http://www.theguardian.com/australia-news/2014/oct/03/abdul-numan-haider-stabbing-policeman-when-he-was-shot-dead-court-hears; AND "Australia: Muslim Who Threatened Prime Minister Stabs Police Officer and Federal Agent, Is Shot Dead," by Robert Spencer, September 23, 2014, Jihad Watch, http://www.jihadwatch.org/2014/09/australia-muslim-who-threatened-prime-minister-stabs-police-officer-and-federal-agent-is-shot-dead

248 September 25, 2014 – beheading/stabbing attacks targeting civilian co-workers; 1 killed, 1 wounded by perpetrator. Perpetrator was just fired from job at Vaughn Foods in Moore, and police allege that he stabbed a co-worker, and then beheaded her with a serrated cooking knife; then he found another co-worker and began stabbing her. A reserve sheriff's deputy who was CEO of the plant shot the perpetrator during the second attack, wounding him. The perpetrator was charged with first-degree murder and prosecutors are seeking the death penalty. The perpetrator recently converted to Islam from Christianity. He reportedly was trying to convert his co-workers to Islam. His Facebook page contains references to Islam, photos of a beheading, men brandishing automatic weapons, and Usama bin Laden. One of his posts read: "She (the Statue of Liberty) is going into flames. She and anybody who's with her." His last post on his Facebook page quoted from 2 Timothy 3:2 of the Bible: "This is the last days," he wrote. The Obama administration has deemed the attack workplace violence. "Oklahoma Beheading: Was it an Act of Terrorism?" by Mark Sappenfield, The Christian Science Monitor, September 28, 2014; AND "'Lock the Door!' 911 Caller Says During Oklahoma Beheading. He Has Stabbed Someone,'" by Lindsey Bever, Washington Post, September 29, 2014, http://www.washingtonpost.com/news/morning-mix/wp/2014/09/29/lock-the-door-911-callers-says-during-oklahoma-beheading-he-has-stabbed-someone; AND "Autopsy Suggests Beheading Victim Fought Back," Associated Press, USA Today, http://www.usatoday.com/story/news/nation/2014/11/26/autopsy-beheading-victim/19564665

249 October 20 and 22, 2014 – car attack and shooting attack, respectively: car attack on soldiers (one in plain clothes), 1 killed, 1 injured by perpetrator; shooting attacks targeting a soldier and afterward parliament, 1 soldier killed by perpetrator: On October 20 – The perpetrator rammed his car into 2 Canadian Forces personnel in the parking lot of the Integrated Personnel Support Centre run by the Veterans Affairs Canada and the Department of Defence in St-Jean-sur-Richelieu, home to the College militaire royal de Saint-Jean university where officers and recruits are trained. He left one of the military personnel with life-threatening injuries to which the victim succumbed, and the second victim with minor injuries. A convert to Islam, the perpetrator purposed to call 911 to inform that he was acting in the name of Allah. He led police on a wild chase until he lost control of his car in a residential area, emerged from the overturned vehicle with a knife, and drew police gunfire, which killed him. Last summer Canadian border authorities seized his passport as he was trying to fly to Turkey to fight with IS. He maintained a Facebook page with photographs of world leaders posing with Jewish leaders, ranted against Jews and Zionists, and cited passages from the Qur'an. His apparent Twitter account indicated that he followed several dozen persons who espoused IS ideals. On October 22 – A perpetrator with a gun fatally shot a military reservist with The Argyll and Sutherland Highlanders of Canada who was standing sentry at the Tomb of the Unknown Soldier at the National War Memorial in Ottawa. The perpetrator was a convert to Islam. Included among the high-risk travellers identified by Canadian intelligence, he had his passport seized to prevent him from joining jihad overseas. After killing the reservist, the perpetrator stormed Parliament Hill, where parliament was in session. The Prime Minister was in the building and rushed to a secure location. A sergeant-at-arms killed the perpetrator after a firefight between the attacker and guards. One parliamentary guard was shot in the leg and another grazed by a bullet. In all, 3 were treated in the hospital and released. The perpetrator appeared on an #ISIS Twitter account, poised for battle, wearing a black and white kiffeyeh. Prime Minister Stephen Harper called it a terror attack. "Canadian Soldiers Run Down in Possible Quebec Terror Attack," by Allen Woods and Bruce Campion=Smith, October 20, 2014, Toronto Star, http://www.thestar.com/news/canada/2014/10/20/stephen_harper_troubled_by_report_o f_possible_terror_attack.html; AND "Homegrown Terror Strikes at Heart of Canada," Michele Mandel, updated October 23, 2014, Toronto Sun, http://www.torontosun.com/2014/10/22/canada-under-attack-by-homegrown-terrorists

250 October 23, 2014 – ax attack targeting police officers; 2 wounded, one critically, but released: The perpetrator, a Muslim convert and proponent of "black power," lurked in the heart of the business district in Jamaica, Queens as he studied his targets, removed an 18" hatchet from his backpack, lunged toward 4 rookie officers who were posing for a picture for a freelance photographer, and then executed his attack. The perpetrator's first swing reportedly broke one of the police officer's arm, the second swing missed, and the third

struck him in the back of the head, fracturing his skull. Another police officer was sliced on the arm during the attack. Two police officers avoided the ax and fatally shot the perpetrator, and a stray bullet struck a woman in the back. The police officers were released from the hospital, and the officer with the skull injury was undergoing therapy, while the woman remained hospitalized. The perpetrator's Facebook page reportedly featured a passage from the Qur'an, a jihadist with a turban and sword taken from a book on Islamic culture in the Iberian Peninsula, and he viewed propaganda and recruitment videos from IS, AQ, and Al-Shabaab, and watched beheading videos. The perpetrator reportedly called for guerilla warfare and a revolution against the U.S. "Pro-ISIS Muslim Convert in NYPD Ax Attack Called for Jihad," by Selim Algar, Shawn Cohen, and Larry Celona, October 24, 2014, New York Post, http://nypost.com/2014/10/24/man-who-struck-cop-with-ax-supported-isis; AND "Terror Connection Not Ruled Out in Hatchet Attack, Police Say," Fox News, October 24, 2014, http://www.foxnews.com/us/2014/10/24/ax-attack-terror-connection; AND "NYPD Hatchet Victim Leaves Queens Hospital to Cheers of Fellow Officers," by Edgar Sandoval and Bill Hutchinson, October 29, 2014, New York Daily News, http://www.nydailynews.com/new-york/nyc-crime/nypd-hatchet-victim-leaves-queens-hospital-article-1.1991958

251 October 31, 2014 – ax attack targeting police officer in Washington D.C.; 1 wounded by perpetrator, who escaped: Just one week after the Queens, New York ax attack on four police officers, a perpetrator with a long-handled ax ambushed a police officer in a patrol cruiser at around 3:20 a.m. on Halloween. The perpetrator bashed his weapon into the driver's side window of the patrol cruiser, partially smashing the safety glass. The weapon remained lodged in the glass where the officer was sitting, however the police officer was not injured during the actual assault. The police officer pursued the perpetrator and sustained non-life threatening injuries during the struggle that ensued, but the perpetrator escaped. The perpetrator is apparently still at large, according to a check of open sources on January 13, 2015. The DC Police Union blog, maintained by the Fraternal Order of Police, Metropolitan Police Department Labor Committee, posted on November 14, 2014 that police were still searching for the suspect. The FBI Unknown Suspects database turned up nothing. "Ax-wielding Attacker on Loose After Assault on Washington, D.C. Cop as NYPD Remains 'Vigilant,'" by Rocco Parascandola and Sasha Goldstein, October 31, 2014, New York Daily News, http://www.nydailynews.com/news/crime/ax-wielding-attacker-loose-assault-article-1.1994117; AND The DC Police Union blog, http://dcpoliceunion.com/blog

252 December 15-16, 2014 (Sydney) – hostage situation involving 1 gunman at Lindt chocolate café in business district, 1 of 10 hostages shot by gunman, 2 hostages died protecting other hostages during police raid in which 1 police officer and hostage-taker killed. Four hostages were injured. "Victims of Sydney Siege Hailed as Heroes After They Die Protecting Hostages," by Josie Ensor and Jonathan Pearlman, December 15, 2014,

ttp://www.telegraph.co.uk/news/worldnews/australiaandthepacific/australia/11295658/
Victims-of-Sydney-siege-hailed-as-heroes-after-they-die-protecting-hostages.html

253 December 20, 2014 – shooting attack, 2 police officers killed, perpetrator killed himself: Two
police officers working overtime as part of an anti-terrorism drill in the Bedford-Stuyvesant
housing project of Brooklyn were targeted by perpetrator, who took up a shooting stance
and shot them "execution-style," point-blank in the head as they sat in their critical response
patrol vehicle. Police responding to the attack chased the perpetrator as he fled to a nearby
subway entrance, and onto a subway platform where he fatally shot himself in the head. The
perpetrator was a fugitive even before the attack; suspected in the shooting death of his ex-
girlfriend in Baltimore hours before. Three hours before the police attack, the perpetrator, a
Muslim, had posted anti-police threats on his Instagram page. A bulletin alerting police of the
threats was just being disseminated at the time of the attack. The perpetrator's Facebook
page featured a photo of the Qur'an open to 8:60, which refers to striking terror into the
enemies of Allah. Note: Article 151 of the Constitution of Iran quotes this same verse.
"Gunman Executes 2 NYPD Cops in Garner 'Revenge,'" by Larry Celona, Shawn Cohen, Jamie
Schram, Amber Jamieson, and Laura Italiano, December 20, 2014,
http://nypost.com/2014/12/20/2-nypd-cops-shot-execution-style-in-brooklyn; AND "Two
NYPD Cops' Assassinated' in Brooklyn Ambush," by Dean Schabner, December 21, 2015, ABC
News, http://abcnews.go.com/US/nypd-cops-assassinated-brooklyn-
ambush/story?id=27738835&singlePage=true; AND "The NYPD Cop-Killing: The Chickens
Come Home to Roost," by Robert Spencer, December 23, 2014, Frontpage Magazine,
http://www.frontpagemag.com/2014/robert-spencer/the-nypd-cop-killing-the-chickens-
come-home-to-roost

254 January 7-9, 2015 – Jan. 7 (Paris): two gunmen with hit list targeting editor, top cartoonists,
police officer inside editorial boardroom of magazine Charlie Hebdo and police officer
outside of building, leaving 12 dead; perpetrators killed in firefight with police at a printing
warehouse in Dammartin-en-Goele where they held a hostage; Jan. 8 (Montrouge, southern
Paris): 1 policewoman investigating traffic accident killed by gunman involved in Jan 9
incident (follows), 1 civilian at the scene seriously wounded after also being shot; Jan 9:
(Paris) hostage-taking situation, gunman targets Hyper Casher kosher supermarket on a
Friday, 4 killed by perpetrator. Perpetrator killed by police. Conflicting reports about
perpetrator's common law wife, alleged to be an accomplice, but who left France for Syria
before the incident. Jan. 7-9 incidents linked.

255 For interesting reading on this subject, see the booklet published in 2004 by the Imam
Khomeini Cultural Center. The booklet examines the religious meaning of jihad, and given
that it was seized from a Hizb'allah stronghold in Maroun al-Ras nearby Israel's northern
border, experts have determined that it might be used as an authoritative ideological

guidebook. The booklet can be accessed at: The Intelligence and Terrorism Information Center, " 'Exporting' the Radical Ideology of the Islamic Revolution in Iran: Analysis of a Booklet Entitled, 'Al-Jihad' (holy war) Found in the Possession of Hezbollah Operatives During the Second Lebanon War. The Booklet Presents the Islamic Teachings of Khamenei, an Ideology Based on Jihad and Shahada (martyrdom for the sake of Allah)," http://www.terrorism-info.org.il/data/pdf/PDF_06_253_2.pdf

256 A. Mikaberidze (Ed.), Conflict and conquest in the Islamic world: A historical encyclopedia (Vol. 1, pp. xxxv-lxxi

257 For instance, challenges to the caliphate ruled by the fourth and final "rightly guided caliph", 'Ali ibn Abu Talib, presented during the Battle of the Camel in Basra, Iraq, in 656 CE; and during the Battle of Siffin in what is now Syria, in 657 CE. H. A. Amin, "The origins of the Sunni/Shia split in Islam," 2001, http://cdn.preterhuman.net/texts/religion.occult.new_age/Islam/The%20Origins%20of%2 0the%20Sunni-Shia%20split%20in%20Islam.pdf; AND British Broadcasting Corporation, "Sunni and Shi'a," updated August 19, 2009, http://www.bbc.co.uk/religion/religions/islam/subdivisions/sunnishia_1.shtml; AND Christopher M. Blanchard, "Islam: Sunnis and Shiites," Congressional Research Service Rep. No. RS21745, January 28, 2009, http://www.fas.org/irp/crs/RS21745.pdf

258 For instance, Sahih Muslim, considered by Muslims to be one of the most reliable hadiths, in book 041, hadith 7015, makes reference to the Muslim antichrist, called the Dajjal. According to this hadith: "He would appear on the way between Syria and Iraq and would spread mischief right and left." The Shi'a believe that their mahdi, or messiah's appearance will accompany tumultuous events that include a great battle involving Sofyani, considered a descendant of the Islamic prophet Muhammad's archenemy, Aub Sofyan, who will seize Syria and Iraq, and will slaughter people bearing the names of the "infallible" Shi'a imams. The mahdi will send troops to kill Sofyani in Beit ol-Moqaddas or Jerusalem. Hadith Collection, Sahih Muslim, Sahih Muslim Book 041, Hadith Number 7015, http://www.hadithcollection.com/sahihmuslim/169-Sahih%20Muslim%20Book%2041.%20Turmoil%20And%20Portents%20Of%20The%20La st%20Hour/15281-sahih-muslim-book-041-hadith-number-7015.html; AND Middle East Media Research Institute. (2007). Waiting for the Mahdi – Official Iranian eschatology outlined in public broadcasting program in Iran [Excerpts from transcript, Special Dispatch No. 1436], http://www.memri.org/report/en/print2021.htm

259 For instance – The U.S. Department of Defense Chapters 4-7 addresses, inter alia, the terrorist threat; threat analysis; legal considerations; and counter-terrorism doctrine: http://www.fas.org/irp/doddir/dod/jp3_07_2.pdf. The Canadian Anti-terrorism Act Bill C 36, Part 1 addresses, inter alia, terror-related conspiracy and terrorism on aircrafts:

http://www.parl.gc.ca/HousePublications/Publication.aspx?DocId=2330950&Lang
uage=e&Mode=1&File=29 Other valuable sources include, but are not limited to: U.S. Patriot
Act, 2001; U.S. Homeland Security Act, 2002; UN Charter, 1945; and UN Resolution 1373,
2001.

260 Those engaging in counter-da'wa campaigns should be aware that the Internal Jihad also
serves as an avenue to develop within Muslims a superior mindset, and to train them to
divorce themselves from the love of humanity and from anything that is un-Islamic. The
Internal Jihad is thus a very subtle, deliberately ambiguous, and a dangerous preparatory
step for desensitizing Muslims to anyone or anything un-Islamic, which, unchecked by
correct moral teaching and standards, leads to the dehumanization of the non-Muslim
"enemy," Muslim "apostates," and anyone that stands in the way of Islam's determined
advance. This indoctrination process is based on Allah's dictates per Qur'anic texts, and on
examples set by Muhammad. It is consistently reinforced by Muslim spiritual guides and
political leaders; and by propaganda that blames Islam's sins on corrupt Western influences,
and that capitalizes on a culture of "victimization" that encourages Muslims to invalidate
Western counter-terrorism campaigns. This is why Muslim terrorists feel fully justified for
their brutal acts, because they are, indeed, faithfully carrying out the dictates of Allah; and
many of them have been convinced that they are sacrificing themselves for Muslim honor
and for an Islamic utopia that has no room for anything non-Islamic.

261 The following material, for example, may effectively be used in a counter-da'wa:

"Narrated by Abu Huraira: Allah's Apostle said, 'I have been sent with the shortest
expressions bearing the widest meanings, and I have been made victorious with terror (cast
in the hearts of the enemy), and while I was sleeping, the keys of the treasures of the world
were brought to me and put in my hand.' Abu Huraira added: 'Allah's Apostle has left the
world and now you, people, are bringing out those treasures (i.e. the Prophet did not benefit
by them).' " Sahih Bukhari, Vol. 4, book 52, hadith no. 220. Christians could point out that the
treasures of the world heaped upon Muhammad were utterly rejected by Jesus, considered
by Muslims to be an Islamic prophet:

"Again, the devil took him to a very high mountain and showed him all the kingdoms of the
world and their splendor. 'All this I will give you,' he said, 'if you will bow down and worship
me.' Jesus said to him, 'Away from me, Satan! For it is written: 'Worship the Lord your God,
and serve him only.' " Matthew 4:8-10.

The following Scripture could then open the door to explaining what Jesus – Yahu'Shua: a
Jew – did to receive a far more consequential set of keys:

"I am the Living One; I was dead, and now look, I am alive for ever and ever! And I hold the
keys of death and Hades." Revelation 1:18

262 Allah began as a generic compound word derived from two Arabic words: al = the + ilah = (any) god/deity. Arabs of differing tribes were using the compound word al-lah to refer to their particular high gods long before the emergence of Islam. Muhammad formalized the composition, making it a proper noun – Allah – and attached it specifically to the male deity most venerated by his Quraysh tribe. This high ancient male deity was believed to have three lower intercessory goddess daughters, al-Lat, al-Uzza and Manat, or the Sun, Venus and Fortune, all esteemed by the Quraysh tribe. Muhammad's relatives named themselves after these deities, and he sacrificed to Al-Uzza. Muhammad placed the male deity favored by his tribe at the top of the pantheon of deities, and exalted it to lord of the Ka'bah, an ancient mega spiritual center and shrine in Mecca associated with the Nabatean male moon deity Hub-al. In all, at least 360 Arabian deities that the Quraysh tribe had guardianship over were worshiped at this temple before and during Muhammad's lifetime. Muhammad delegitimized all the other deities in the pantheon at this temple in order to ensure that his tribe's male deity was supreme; and today, the Ka'bah is used for the Hajj and is a key terrorism fundraising destination. Muhammad also asserted that his deity, Allah, had begotten no offspring, however in his quest to win over other tribal members to his new religion, he vacillated by incorporating the deity's three goddess daughters into a revelation: "These are the swans exalted; whose intercession is to be hoped for; have ye considered Al-Lat and Al-Uzza, and the third, Manat, the other?" The revelation, recorded in Qur'an 53:19, but eventually removed, caused a great falling away from Islam, with many denouncing the religion. Muhammad's religion, nevertheless, took root among the unschooled Arab masses, and Allah became central to the state-sponsored religious system of the Arab empire. The crescent moon – still the preeminent icon of Islam today – appeared on ancient Islamic coins, and on flags, and atop mosques and minarets. Muhammad's false narrative regarding his deity was given further credence as Bible translators producing the Arabic Bible as an alternative to the Qur'an errantly substituted the name Allah wherever Elohim, a uniquely Hebrew reference to God, appeared: a condition imposed upon them during their quest to bring the Bible to Arabic speaking audiences. Today, particularly in the West, Muslims assert that Allah is simply another name for the Judeo-Christian God; accordingly, they peddle the counterfeit narrative that Allah and God are the same, and very persistently use them interchangeably. Through their persistence, and because Islam takes on an air of sanctity attained by plagiarizing and distorting Biblical texts, Muslims have trained Westerners to follow suit, such that Muhammad's deity is uncritically equated with the God of the Hebrews spoken of in the Bible. According to Exodus 3:15, God's memorial name "forever" is "Elohe Avraham, Elohe Yizhaq vElohe Ya'aqov" or the God of Abraham, the God of Isaac and the God of Jacob, which is a confirmation of the eternal covenant that God has with the Jews, passed down through these three Biblical figures. It is this covenant relationship that draws intense Muslim hatred of Jews, and this hatred fuels the flames of jihad. "Revolutionary Islam and the

Arab-Israeli Conflict: Connecting the Dots," by Sandra Warmoth, excerpts from a March 2009 report sent to political and religious leaders in the U.S. and abroad.

263 Muslims assure Westerners that Muhammad did not force his religion upon anyone. They frequently cite Qur'an 2:256, which reads: "There is no compulsion in religion. The right direction is henceforth distinct from error. And he who rejecteth false deities and believeth in Allah hath grasped a firm handhold which will never break. Allah is Hearer, Knower." However Muslim scholars and jurists; even jihadists, know well that Qur'an 2:256 is a ruse, as it was inserted in the interest of deflecting the fact that Muhammad, indeed, ordered disciples to set on fire men and their homes if the latter failed to show up for prayer. For example, Sahi Bukhari, Vol 1. Book 11, Hadith 626 reads: "Narrated Abu Huraira: 'The Prophet said, "No prayer is harder for the hypocrites than the Fajr and the 'Isha' prayers and if they knew the reward for these prayers at their respective times, they would certainly present themselves (in the mosques) even if they had to crawl." The Prophet added, "Certainly I decided to order the Mu'adh-dhin (call- maker) to pronounce Iqama and order a man to lead the prayer and then take a fire flame to burn all those who had not left their houses so far for the prayer along with their houses." ' " Also, Sahi Bukhari, Vol. 1, Book 11, Hadith 617 reads: "Narrated Abu Huraira: 'Allah's Apostle said, "By Him in Whose Hand my soul is I was about to order for collecting fire-wood (fuel) and then order someone to pronounce the Adhan for the prayer and then order someone to lead the prayer then I would go from behind and burn the houses of men who did not present themselves for the (compulsory congregational) prayer. By Him, in Whose Hands my soul is, if anyone of them had known that he would get a bone covered with good meat or two (small) pieces of meat present in between two ribs, he would have turned up for the 'Isha' prayer." ' " Also, Sahi Bukhari, Vol. 1, Book 11, Hadith 602 reads: "Narrated Abu Dhar: 'We were in the company of the Prophet on a journey and the Mu'adhdhin wanted to pronounce the Adhan for the (Zuhr) prayer. The Prophet said to him, "Let it become cooler." Then he again wanted to pronounce the Adhan but the Prophet; said to him, "Let it become cooler." The Mu'adh-dhin again wanted to pronounce the Adhan for the prayer but the Prophet said, "Let it become cooler," till the shadows of the hillocks become equal to their sizes. The Prophet added, "The severity of the heat is from the raging of Hell." ' "

www.ingramcontent.com/pod-product-compliance
Lightning Source LLC
Chambersburg PA
CBHW022343290526
45786CB00014B/2385